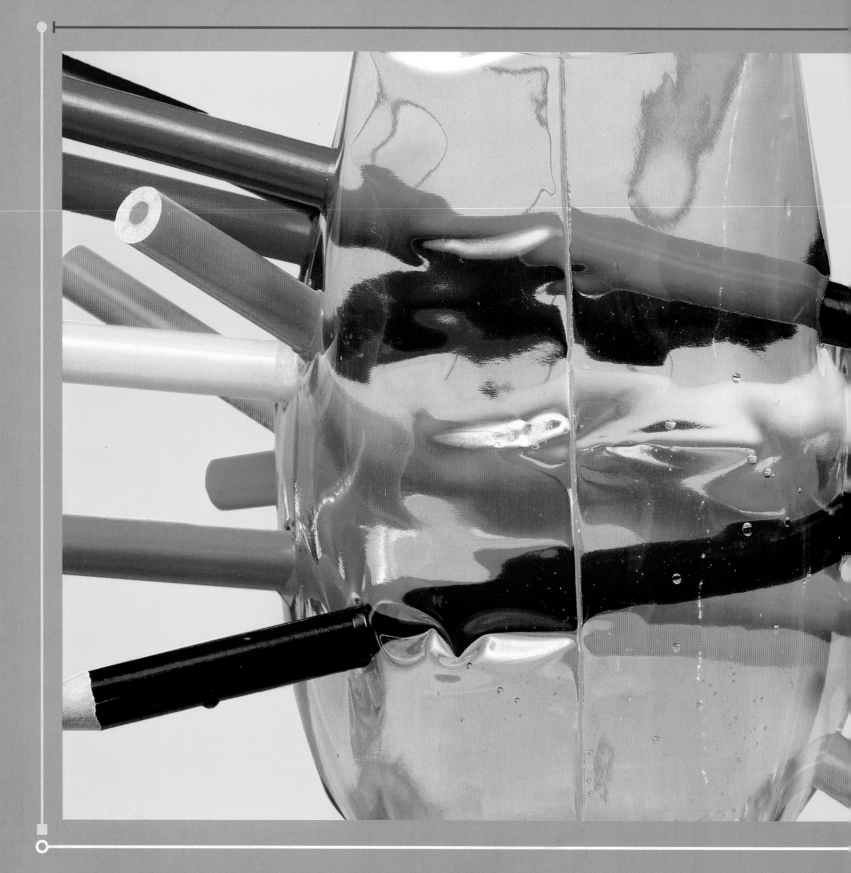

MAKER GENIUS

◾SCHOLASTIC

**New York Toronto London Auckland
Sydney Mexico City New Delhi Hong Kong**

SCHOLASTIC

New York Toronto London Auckland
Sydney Mexico City New Delhi Hong Kong

Consultants:

Olga Markoulides MA (Oxon)
David Ellington BSc

ISBN 978-1-338-29195-7

10 9 8 7 6 5 4 3 2 1   17 18 19 20 21

Printed in Shenzhen, China
First edition, January 2019

CONTENTS

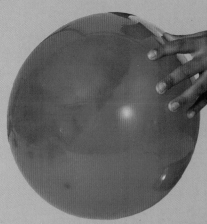

⭐ 12 ACTIONS AND REACTIONS

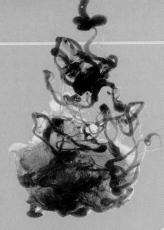

MAKER SCIENCE

When you play a tune on the cover of this book, you are being a musician (maybe!) But you are also being a scientist. By pressing the cover buttons you are creating a circuit, and the power is coming from a battery. But did you know you can use real bananas to power up a light bulb? In fact, you can use lemons, limes, and oranges, too.

Gooey, stringy slime

WHAT IS SCIENCE

The amazing thing about science is that it's everywhere. Wherever you look there's science at work, and play. Because of science we have computers and cars, satellites and submarines. All serious stuff. But science can also be about slime, flying eggs, lava lamps, fizzy volcanos, and bath bombs, and that's all really serious, and often messy, fun. So roll up your scientific sleeves and dive into some amazing experiments. And along the way, come to grips with gravity,

grow some geodes, float your boat, create an eruption, and reveal some secret messages. And for every experiment you do there are always ways to hack away at more science by trying some new ideas of your own.

MAKER GENIUS!

Maker science is all about creating and inventing as the best way to find out. Make these awesome projects, remake them differently, test them, tinker with them and discover something new time after time. This book shows you how to have some super fun with science.

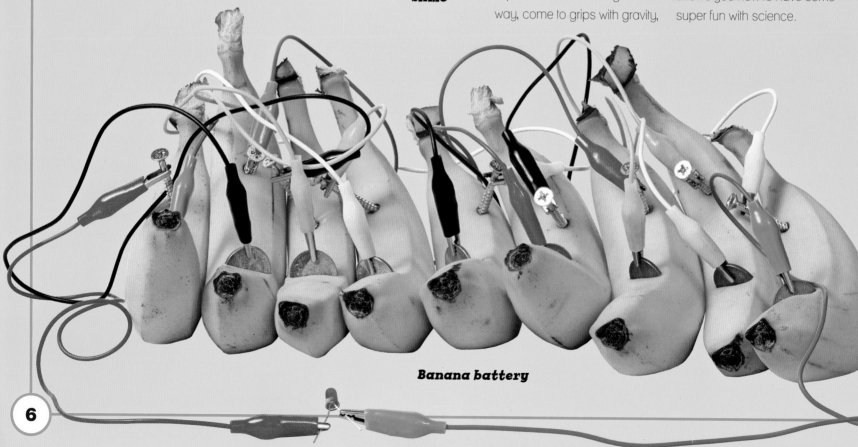

Banana battery

Underwater volcano

Chemical reactions

Elements and life

Sunlight to gas

Thick and thin liquids

GET EXPERIMENTAL

Bean shoots

Scientists throughout history were simply curious. They wanted to learn why, how, when, what. So they tinkered. They started with something they knew about and added, changed, prodded, blew up, etc. Experiments failed along the way as much as they succeeded, but each time they learned something new. Nothing has changed today. Many inventions come about by tinkering with something and creating something entirely surprising. That's what this book is about.

YOU ARE A SCIENTIST...

The more you hack, the more you learn, and who knows, you may discover something no one has discovered before! When you experiment you can take ordinary objects and materials and make the impossible possible. Give it a try!

Frozen science

Colorful solutions

MAKER MATERIALS

To be a maker science genius, you're going to need some materials to do your experiments with, right? Do you think that sounds like it's going to get complicated? Well, it isn't! You'll be surprised how many science experiments you can do with some really basic stuff that you probably already have at home.

Jungle jar

WHAT YOU NEED

Sometimes the simplest experiments are the most rewarding, especially if it's really easy to find the things you need to get started. If you can get ahold of some cardboard, tape, recycled containers, paper towel, eggs, pencils, trash bags, string, and water—and most likely you can—then you already have a science starter kit at your disposal. Check out the What You Need lists that accompany each experiment, get everything ready, and you are on your way.

BE A SAFE SCIENTIST

- ☐ Always ask for an adult's permission before using household materials.

- ☐ Get an adult to help you if instructions involve using a microwave, stove or other heat source.

- ☐ Cover any flat work surface to protect it, especially if ingredients that stain, like food coloring, are being used.

- ☐ Avoid contact with eyes where appropriate.

- ☐ Discontinue if you have any skin or eye irritation.

- ☐ Wash your hands with soapy water after each experiment.

- ☐ Store any slime in an airtight container.

- ☐ Put away your ingredients after use. This is especially important if your experiment involves perishable ingredients, like milk.

- ☐ Dispose of used ingredients carefully. Wash liquids down the sink, and put solids in a plastic bag and place in the trash.

Glowing egg

Fruit skins

Balloons and pressure

Oil and water

Metal wire and electricity

Magnets and metals

HOW TO USE THIS BOOK

Conducting science experiments can often mean some mess and mayhem, so remember to wear suitable clothing! Then all you have to do is follow the instructions. Remember to learn from the science and be bold enough to try new things. Scientists never stop tinkering, hacking, and learning. Have fun!

WHAT YOU NEED

15 minutes

- ☐ 3 raw eggs
- ☐ white vinegar
- ☐ jar

1 First check out what you need for the experiment. It's always easier if you prepare the equipment first.

2 The time circle tells you how long you will need to complete the experiment. Some take a few days, but are worth the wait!

3 The bananas show how tricky an experiment can be. The more bananas, the more difficult it may be. Try an easy one first!

The experiments are divided into four sections that follow a specific theme.

Watch out for me! I give you top tips throughout the book. Do what I tell you and you won't go wrong!

Watch out for me! I tell you when you need an adult to help you.

Read the instructions carefully before you start.

TOP TIP

SCIENCE

NOW HACK IT!!

⭐ TRY IT!

Once you've completed the experiment, you may not want to stop! The "Hack its" give you ideas to tinker, pull apart, swap, fiddle, and generally hack the experiment to take it further.

THE SCIENCE STUFF

WHY?

It's all very well doing the experiment, but it's also important that you understand why it works. Read "The Science Stuff" to understand the amazing science behind the cool experiments.

4 Follow the step-by-step instructions carefully. Take your time—don't rush or you may mess up! Use the pictures to help you, too.

FUN WITH SCIENCE!

5 The "Multi-experiment" pages give you more experiments based on a common theme, such as water, plants, or eggs.

Make sure you read all the text around the page. There are hints and tips everywhere!

Even the multi-experiments have "Hack its!"

ACTIONS AND REACTIONS

CHEMICAL REACTIONS

The chemical side of science can often be the most exciting and sometimes most explosive part. A chemical reaction is when one or more substances form something completely new and different. The starting materials are called "reactants" and what you end up with are called the "products." You know a chemical reaction has taken place if you can see or feel a change—for example; a color change, change in temperature, light is given out, fizzing, or change of texture. Some chemical reactions are slow and others are explosively fast. Rusting happens very slowly and is the reaction between iron and oxygen in the air. An acid reacting with a carbonate (like vinegar and baking soda) happens very quickly and you see fizzing straight away. Get ready for some fizzing, bubbling, expanding, freezing, slimy, bouncing fun!

CHEMICAL REACTIONS...

Chemical reactions happen all around us and are very important in everyday life. The medicines we take to improve our health are made using chemical reactions. All plastics that we use are made through chemical reactions as are other materials such as glass, metal alloys used in cars, and human-made fibers such as polyester and nylon.

BATH FIZZ...

Who would have thought that combining some simple kitchen ingredients could create a chemical reaction in your bath? Try the explosive fizzing bath bomb experiment.

Watch out, this chapter can get explosive!

TOP TIP

ACIDS AND BASES...

Acids are a group of chemicals that are found all over the place and tend to taste quite sour, for example citric acid in lemon juice or acetic acid in vinegar. The chemical opposite of an acid is a base and these taste quite soapy and feel slimy e.g. baking soda and dish soap. Acids and bases will react with each other to form a product called a "salt." Carbonates are a type of base and will react with acids to form carbon dioxide as well as a salt.

CABBAGE MAGIC

Find out how cabbage juice can magically turn liquids into rainbows of colors...then decorate a T-shirt with the end products!

SOLVENTS, SOLUTES, AND SOLUTIONS...

A solution is formed when a solute is dissolved into a solvent. For example salt is a solute and will dissolve in water. So water is a solvent to make salty water. Some solutes will only dissolve in certain solvents e.g. salt will easily dissolve in water, but will not dissolve in oil. Nail polish dissolves in nail polish remover, but not in water (which is quite handy).

CABBAGE CHEMISTRY (PART 1)

This experiment is about acids and bases. Most liquids are acids, neutrals, or bases. Scientists use the pH scale to measure how acidic or basic a liquid is. pH is a number from 0-14 with 0 being a strong acid and 14 being an extreme base. Pure water is pH7, which is neutral. How do you tell if something is an acid or a base? You can use a substance called an indicator. Red cabbage is an indicator—strange, but true! Get ready for some smelly science!

WHAT YOU NEED

- ☐ ½ head of a red cabbage
- ☐ knife
- ☐ blender
- ☐ water
- ☐ large bowl
- ☐ sieve
- ☐ small clear container
- ☐ lemon
- ☐ eye dropper

Have an adult help you chop the cabbage and operate the blender.

TOP TIP

1 Ask an adult to help you cut the red cabbage into small chunks carefully. Put the chunks into the blender.

Drip the drops

16

CABBAGE MAGIC...

Red cabbage juice works as an indicator because it contains the pigment anthocyanin, which changes color when it is mixed with an acid or base. The lemon turns the indicator pink, which shows that the juice is an acid. Look at the scale below. What pH is lemon juice?

RED CABBAGE pH SCALE...

1	3	5	7	9	11	13
ACID			NEUTRAL			BASE

NOW HACK IT!!

⭐ **TRY THIS!**

Want a handy way to test pH levels? Make indicator paper! Here's how. Cut up some strips of coffee filter paper. Soak them in the cabbage indicator. Then remove the strips and leave them to dry. Once dried, dip the strips into different solutions and watch the color of the paper change!

4 Squeeze half the juice of a lemon into a small clear container and add some water. Put a few drops of your indicator into the jar. What happens? Check the indicator scale. Is the lemon an acid or a base?

2 Pour water into the blender until it just covers the cabbage. Close the lid. Have an adult help you turn on the machine. Blend the cabbage until the chunks are chopped up.

3 Pour the mixture through the sieve and into the bowl. The strained cabbage liquid can be used as an indicator!!

and watch the color change...

Science Magic!

CABBAGE CHEMISTRY (PART 2)

Ask an adult if you can test some solutions from around the house to see if they are an acid, a base, or neutral. Try out the examples below—you may need to dissolve some household items in liquid to make solutions. Drop in your cabbage indicator and watch the rainbow of colors begin!

INDICATOR INDICATION...

When you drop the cabbage juice indicator into the solutions, they immediately change color to show whether the solution is an acid or a base. Water is neither an acid nor a base, it is in between and known as neutral. Neutral solutions are blue in a cabbage indicator test. The acids turn pink or red, and the bases turn greeny-yellow. Use the pH scale on page 17 to check your results.

Put the cabbage indicator in first, then drop the fizzy tablet in. Does the liquid change color?

Fizzzz!

Mix the baking soda into the water well before you test it.

White vinegar turns bright red—that's acid!

Water is neutral so will turn blue.

ANTACID TABLET

BAKING SODA

WHITE VINEGAR

Start by putting in one or two drops of cabbage indicator, then add more to see what happens.

TOP TIP

NOW HACK IT!!

⭐ TRY THIS!

Take a paper straw and blow into a cup of your cabbage indicator. The liquid should turn red as the carbon dioxide that you breathe out reacts with the indicator to form carbonic acid.

Lemonade is acidic—just like vinegar!

...what happens?

Water stays neutral when salt is added, but the salt does add chloride ions that change the color.

Detergent is definitely a base! Don't use too much.

Watch the detergent! Does it start out a different color?

TAP WATER   LEMONADE   SALT WATER   DETERGENT

PAINTING WITH CABBAGE

Once you have mastered the science of cabbage indicators, you can use your newfound skill to explore the creative side of acids and bases. Get ready to use your cabbage indicator and different types of liquid to make wearable art! Be sure to ask an adult before experimenting with household liquids.

WHAT YOU NEED

1 hour

- ☐ white, 100% cotton T-shirt
- ☐ large bowl
- ☐ red cabbage indicator (page 16)
- ☐ different types of liquid in individual cups
- ☐ eyedropper or paintbrush

1 Soak a white T-shirt in a bowl of cabbage indicator for ½ an hour. Then squeeze out the liquid and hang the shirt up to dry. Do NOT rinse the shirt in water!

2 Prepare your "paint!" Select at least two different liquids. You could use baking soda solution, detergent, apple juice, or water. Be sure to use at least one acid and one base.

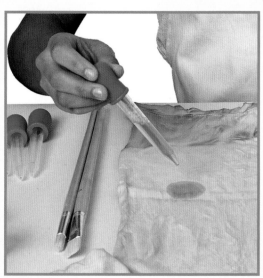

3 Using a dropper or a paintbrush, drip some of the liquids onto the shirt. Squirt some of the acids and bases next to each other. What patterns do they create?

THE SCIENCE STUFF

ACID TEST!

Because the T-shirt has been soaked in cabbage juice, the fabric reacts with the acids and bases in the same way as the cabbage juice did on the previous page. For example, lemon juice turns the indicator pink and detergent turns it green!

NOW HACK IT!!

★ TRY THIS!

Does this experiment work on paper? Soak a piece of white paper in the cabbage indicator and leave it to dry. Try dropping the different solutions to make multi-colored paper.

★ NOW TRY THIS!

Use your T-shirt test to check the water in your area. Test tap water, rainwater, and river or lake water. Are they different, and if so why do you think that is?

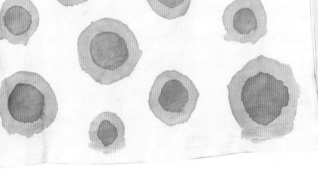

Wear an apron so you don't stain your clothes!

TOP TIP

4 When you have finished, hang the T-shirt up to dry. Don't wash the shirt. If you do, the color will come out. Be sure not to wear it in the rain!

BATH BOMBS

Get ready for some fizzy fun! These "bath bombs" can trigger a chemical reaction in your tub! Choose a great fragrance and your bath will be scent-sational! Not only will it smell good, the color will brighten your bath water and the oil will be good for your skin.

WHAT YOU NEED

4 hours

- ☐ mixing bowl
- ☐ 1 cup (225 g) baking powder
- ☐ 3 tbsp vegetable oil (with a little extra for greasing)
- ☐ 15 drops food coloring
- ☐ 15 drops essential oil (optional—for fragrance)
- ☐ muffin pan
- ☐ spoon

TOP TIP

Don't add the vegetable oil too quickly or it will start to foam!

1 Take a mixing bowl and pour the baking powder into it.

2 Mix the vegetable oil and the food coloring into the baking powder. Add the essential oil if you are using it. The mixture should feel like sand.

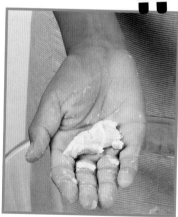

3 When the oil is mixed in, use your hands to knead the mixture together. When it is ready you should be able to squeeze it into a solid.

4 Lightly grease a muffin pan with the extra vegetable oil. Fill each cavity with your mixture, pushing it down with a spoon. Leave the tray in a cool place for 3 to 4 hours.

THE SCIENCE STUFF

DUNK, FIZZ . . . !

When you drop a bomb into the water, it causes a chemical reaction between the baking soda (a base) and the tartaric acid, both of which are ingredients in the baking powder. Acids and bases react with one another. This reaction creates carbon dioxide gas, which forms bubbles and rises to the surface, making the bath bomb fizz like crazy!

NOW HACK IT!!

⭐ TRY THIS!

Experiment with different oils. Does olive oil produce more fizz than vegetable oil? Can you make multi-colored bombs?

⭐ NOW TRY THIS!

If you add rose petals, dried lavender, or glitter, the bath bombs make fantastic presents.

5 When the bath bombs have hardened, carefully lift them out of the pan. Then drop one into the water during your bath time...fizzzzz!

YEAST ALIVE!

You can blow up a balloon without breathing into it. Sounds like magic? The secret of this trick is a tiny ingredient with big air power: yeast! It's the same ingredient used to create the holes in bread. Try this activity to see yeast in action!

Which balloon blows UP the most?

WHAT YOU NEED

1 hour

- ☐ warm water
- ☐ 3 clean bottles
- ☐ 3 tbsp dried yeast
- ☐ 1 tsp honey
- ☐ 2 tsp sugar
- ☐ 3 balloons, same size, but different colors

TOP TIP

Use the balloon colors to help you identify what is in each bottle.

1 Pour warm water into each of the 3 bottles, until each bottle is about a third full.

2 Pour one tbsp of dried yeast into each bottle. Get ready! You have to do the following steps quickly!

3 Put the honey into one bottle. Put the sugar into another bottle. Leave the third bottle as it is.

4 Stretch the neck of a balloon over the mouth of each bottle. Put the bottles in a warm spot. Watch what happens over the next hour.

You can use more than three bottles if you want to blow up more balloons.

NOW HACK IT!!

The banana is used as a different source of sugar. So yeast, mashed banana, and water work in the same way as water, yeast, and sugar.

TRY THIS!

Try putting a mashed, overripe banana into a bottle with yeast and water. Pop a balloon onto the top and leave the bottle on a warm windowsill. What happens?

THE SCIENCE STUFF

SUGAR FIZZ...

Yeasts are microbes. They are tiny living organisms! When the yeast is cold and dry, it is resting. Warm water activates the yeast. Once awake, the yeast eats the sugar (including the sugar in the honey). Eating sugar causes the yeast to release carbon dioxide (CO_2) gas. This gas fills the bottles and then expands into the balloons, too! Take a look at your balloons. Why didn't one inflate? Which of these substances made the yeast more gassy: sugar or honey?

SODA EXPLOSION!

Get your raincoat out. Choose some friends who don't mind getting sticky. Head outside to an open space. Get ready to make one explosive fountain! Who would have thought that a bottle of soda and chewy mints could be such a blast!

15 minutes

WHAT YOU NEED

- ☐ sheet of construction paper
- ☐ tape
- ☐ 1 pack of Mentos mints
- ☐ plastic bottle of diet cola

How tall is your blast? Is it taller than you?

1 Roll up the piece of construction paper, making sure that the mints can fit inside it quite easily. Tape it along the side to make a tube.

2 Drop your mints down the tube. You can start with two or three mints, or maybe you'll be brave enough to try more!

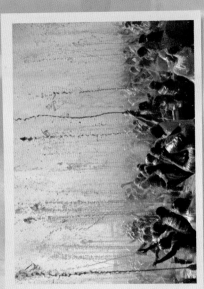

NOW HACK IT!

Make sure the mints drop as quickly as possible!

3 Squeeze the bottom of the tube and hold it above the bottle. When you are ready, let the mints drop into the bottle. Stand far back!

4 After decades of experimenting, scientists have decided that seven mints produce the best results. What do you think?

⭐ TRY THIS!

Different temperatures and sodas might make a difference. Leave a bottle in the fridge overnight before you use it. Then leave a soda bottle in warm water for an hour before you use it.

⭐ BANG!

There has to be a way to create the biggest explosion ever. Look at "Try this!" for some ideas.

SUPER BLAST!
In 2014, a Guiness World Record was set in Mexico. 4,344 minty soda explosions were set off, producing the biggest minty soda explosion of all time!

THE SCIENCE STUFF

EXPLODING BLAST...
Soda is fizzy because it has carbon dioxide (CO_2) gas in it. The gas is trapped in the soda, and can't get out until it is released. The rough surface of the Mentos attracts the CO_2 bubbles. When the candies fall to the bottom of the bottle, bubbles form all around them. This triggers the gas in the soda to rush out of the bottle, forcing the liquid above it up and out of the bottle. Whoooshhh!

27

FIZZY WIGGLY VOLCANO

When a volcano goes KABOOM, out spews fiery, hot lava. This experiment will explode, too! Get ready to build your very own wobbly volcano, and cause an eruption with baking soda and vinegar. You may want to take this experiment outside—it can get pretty messy!

WHAT YOU NEED

5 hours

- ☐ funnel
- ☐ modeling clay
- ☐ vegetable oil
- ☐ jug
- ☐ box of flavored gelatin mix
- ☐ water
- ☐ plate
- ☐ spoon
- ☐ 1 tbsp baking soda
- ☐ cup
- ☐ ½ cup (120 ml) white vinegar
- ☐ 2-3 drops food coloring

Make sure there's enough room to add the vinegar.

TOP TIP

1 Use a small piece of modeling clay to plug the small opening in the funnel. Use your finger to dab some oil on the clay so the gelatin doesn't stick to it.

2 Make some gelatin by following the packet's instructions, but only use half the amount of water. Pour the solution into the funnel and rest it in the jug while the mixture sets.

3 Turn the gelatin out onto a plate. Dig a hole in the top with a spoon to make a "vent." Spoon baking soda into the hole, leaving room at the top.

4 Mix the food coloring with the vinegar in a cup. Pour the colored vinegar into the baking soda.

5 Stand back and watch the eruption!

NOW HACK IT!!

★ TRY THIS!

Add some dish soap to the colored vinegar before pouring the mixture into the volcanic "vent." What does this do to your eruption?

NOW TRY THIS!

Put some coffee grounds into the mixture if you want to add some volcanic "debris!"

THE SCIENCE STUFF

EXPLOSIVE SCIENCE...

The eruption is all to do with chemical reactions. If you mix an acid, like vinegar, with a base, such as baking soda, then you get a reaction. The reaction produces carbon dioxide (CO_2) gas, which is lighter than the baking soda and the vinegar. The pressure builds up and forces the mixture to froth over the top.

IN THE REAL WORLD...

Volcanoes erupt because of density and pressure, just like your gelatin version. The molten rock, called magma, is lighter than the surrounding rock. The pressure forces the magma to the surface and it bursts out as lava!

FUN WITH QUICK REACTIONS

2 Pour some white vinegar into a bowl, add 1 tsp salt, and stir. Put about five dirty, dull-looking pennies in the bowl and slowly count to ten. Take the pennies out and rinse them with water. What do they look like now?

With a little bit of science know-how, you can create some awesome reactions. Try these simple, speedy experiments that will amaze, explode, and shine!

WHO KNEW?

Your pennies should be shiny and look as good as new! The acid in the vinegar reacts with the salt to remove copper oxide, which was making your pennies look dull.

1

DANCING RAISINS

Fill up three glasses with different types of soda. Drop 15–20 raisins in each glass. What happens? What happens if you use pasta or dried beans instead of raisins?

WHO KNEW?

Raisins are more dense than water, so they sink. (Find out all about density on page 69). Raisins have a wrinkly surface that carbon dioxide (CO_2) bubbles get attached to. As more gas bubbles attach to a raisin, the whole lump becomes less dense than its surrounding water. So the raisin gets lifted upward with the bubbles.

Raisins in fizzy water

Raisins in orange soda

Pasta and beans in fizzy water

3 UNDERWATER VOLCANO

Cut a long piece of string. Tie it around the neck of a small bottle. Pour cold water into a large, clear container until it is about three-quarters full. Fill the bottle with warm water—make sure it's not too hot. Add food coloring to turn the water red. Use the string to lower the small bottle into the large container. What happens?

WHO KNEW?

Red water rises from the bottle, like an underwater volcano. The red water rises because hot water is less dense than cold water. The molecules in hot water have more energy so move more and move faster than water particles that are cold. This means that the average distance between hot water particles is bigger than the average distance between cold water particles. This makes hot water less dense than cold water.

4 SELF-EXPLODING BAG

Ask an adult to help you put ¼ cup (60 ml) of quite warm water into a sealable plastic bag and add ½ cup (120 ml) of vinegar. Then zip up the bag. Put 3 tsps of baking soda powder in the middle of a thin piece of tissue. Wrap the tissue around the powder. Then partially open the bag and drop in the tissue packet. Put the bag on the ground, give it a little shake, and stand far back! What happens?

WHO KNEW?

The bag will start to expand, and should go POP! As you read earlier, combining baking soda and vinegar causes a chemical reaction that creates CO_2. This gas starts to fill the bag. When there becomes too much gas for the bag to hold . . . POP!

INVISIBLE INK

If you want to write a secret message, you need to make some invisible ink! It's so simple, all you need is a lemon and a chemical reaction! Strain the lemon juice into a bowl to remove the pulp and seeds. Add two or three drops of water and mix. Use a paintbrush dipped in the lemon to write a secret message onto white paper. Leave it to dry and the juice will disappear. To get your message back, ask an adult to iron the sheet of paper under a piece of thin fabric. Try it, but shhhh, don't tell anyone what you reveal!

30 minutes

WHAT YOU NEED

- ☐ lemon
- ☐ bowl
- ☐ strainer
- ☐ water
- ☐ paintbrush
- ☐ white paper
- ☐ iron or hairdryer

Ask someone to help with the iron or hairdryer!

TOP TIP

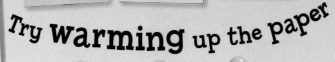

Try **warming** up the paper

with a **hairdryer** . . .

. . . what **happens?**

NOW HACK IT!!

★ **TRY THIS!**

Do other substances work instead of lemon juice? Try using milk or vinegar.

★ **NOW TRY THIS!**

Mix ¼ cup (43 g) of baking soda with ¼ cup (60 ml) of water. Use the paste to write a message on white paper. When the message is dry rub it with grape juice. Baking soda (a base) and grape juice (an acid) react with each other in an acid-base reaction, producing a color change in the paper.

THE
SCIENCE
STUFF

GET THE MESSAGE...?

Lemon juice contains carbon compounds. These substances are colorless at room temperature. Things change when you apply heat. Heat can break down carbon compounds, releasing the carbon. When the carbon comes in contact with oxygen in the air, a chemical reaction called oxidation occurs. It causes the carbon to turn brown.

TATTOO A BANANA!

We've all seen bananas go brown. Now you can use that to your advantage and tattoo a banana! If you want to draw something very complex, draw a picture on parchment paper first and place it on your banana to guide you where to tattoo. When you've mastered the art, surprise your family by leaving banana messages or crazy banana drawings in your fruit bowl!

Make sure you use a banana that hasn't turned brown yet.

TOP TIP

WHAT YOU NEED

- ☐ yellow banana
- ☐ toothpick

10 minutes

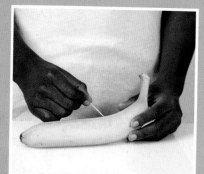

1 Use a toothpick to pierce holes in a banana skin. The holes you pierce will go brown quite quickly. You can also scratch the surface to turn a whole area black.

Strong block shapes.

Trace images with a pencil before you use the toothpick for more detailed designs.

What will you tattoo?

THE SCIENCE STUFF

GO BANANAS...!

Bananas contain chemicals including one called polyphenol oxidase. When you pierce the skin, this causes the cells to split and the polyphenol oxidase causes a reaction to happen between oxygen in the air and other chemicals in the banana, which results in brown chemicals eventually being made. This reaction is called oxidization.

NOW HACK IT!!

⭐ TRY THIS!

Try poking the stick through to the banana inside. Does the tattoo also go through to the banana? What happens if you leave the banana for a week?

BOUNCING EGGS!

What happens when you drop an uncooked egg onto the ground? Splat! Not pretty. What if there is a way to turn a raw egg into a bouncy ball? Take a crack at this activity to learn how!

WHAT YOU NEED

3 days

- ☐ clean glass jar with a lid
- ☐ 3 raw eggs
- ☐ white vinegar
- ☐ large plate

Don't drop the eggs from too high up to start with!

TOP TIP

1 Place the eggs into the jar. Pour in the white vinegar until the eggs are completely covered.

2 Observe what happens to the eggs. Do you see bubbles?

3 After three days, lift the eggs out of the jar. Do they feel rubbery? The shells have disappeared! Gently rinse the eggs under warm tap water to remove any shell residue.

4 Take one of the eggs and hold it up to the light. Can you see the egg yolk? Turn the egg around in your hand. Can you see the yolk moving around?

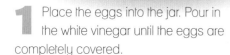

NOW HACK IT!!

TRY IT!

Leave one of the eggs in vinegar for three extra days. Does the egg swell? The vinegar has more water particles in it than the inside of the egg. To balance this, water molecules move from the vinegar into the egg through the semi-permeable membrane. This is known as osmosis.

DYE IT!

Make some more eggs to repeat this experiment with other colors. Put the eggs into a bowl of tap water and add 10 drops of food coloring. How long does it take for the egg to change color?

THE SCIENCE STUFF

ACID TEST...

The eggshell is made of calcium carbonate, which is insoluble in water. The shell reacts with the acetic acid in the vinegar to make a different chemical (a salt), which is soluble in water. So the shell reacts with the acid and then the product of that reaction dissolves, and carbon dioxide gets released. (That's the gas bubbles you saw in step 2!) Why doesn't the rest of the egg fall apart? Just under the shell is a membrane. This protective layer is thin and stretchy. It's also tough up to a certain point. This allows you to bounce the egg—but lightly!

5 Bring an egg to about 1 inch (2.5 cm) above a flat surface (or a plate). Drop the egg. Does it bounce? Now try dropping the egg from a bit higher up. Keep going higher. At what point does your egg go splat?

Try dropping it from higher and higher! . . . what happens?

EGG-CITING EGGS-TRAORDINARY EGGS!

There is more to eggs than meets the eye. Find out why they are "egg" shaped. Make eggs glow, and watch them sink and float. Then see how they can magically squeeze into a bottle!

1

EGG ROLL

Take a round ball and an egg. Roll them both on the floor. How do they roll? Do they behave differently? Why do you think that is?

WHO KNEW?

The ball moves easily around the floor. The egg rolls a little, but mostly just wobbles. The oval shape of a birds' egg stops it from rolling out of the nest. The shape also helps make the eggs less likely to crack.

2

EGG IN A BOTTLE

!!! You will need an adult to help you with this experiment because it uses boiling water and candles. Find a bottle that an egg cannot fit into. Boil an egg for 10 minutes. Peel off the shell and stick two candles into the pointy end. Light the candles and hold the egg just under the neck of the upside-down bottle for a minute to heat it up. Then with a quick action, push the egg up to the neck and watch it suck up!

WHO KNEW?

The candles heat the inside of the bottle causing the molecules in the air to drift apart and escape down through the opening. When the egg reaches the neck and the candles go out, the air in the bottle cools down forcing the molecules to gather closer together again and making room for new air molecules. No air can get in so instead the egg is squeezed upward into the bottle!

EGG IN A SPIN

Take two eggs, one hard-boiled (but cool) and one raw. Spin the eggs and watch what happens.

WHO KNEW?

The hard-boiled egg spins for longer. The liquid inside the raw egg slides about and stops the egg from spinning as fast. Now slow the eggs with your finger. The hard-boiled egg stops quickly. The raw egg keeps turning because the liquid inside keeps turning.

FLOATING EGG

Fill two glasses with water. Add salt to one of the glasses and stir until dissolved. Pop an egg into each glass and watch what happens.

WHO KNEW?

The egg in regular water sinks because the egg is denser than the water. Salt makes water more dense. So if enough salt is mixed in water, the egg will float!

GIANT GLOWING EGG!

Dissolve an eggshell in vinegar for three days as per the bouncing eggs (page 36). Ask an adult to help you cut open a non-toxic highlighter pen and remove the colored foam strip. Squeeze the ink out of the strip into a bowl of water. Submerge the egg in the bowl. Leave overnight. Does the egg glow?

WHO KNEW?

As on page 36, the shell has dissolved in the vinegar leaving the membrane. There are more water molecules outside the egg than inside, so the molecules move through the membrane into the egg. The colored molecules move into the egg along with the water molecules.

GLITTERING GEODES

A geode is a hollow rock lined with crystals inside. Geodes take millions of years to form. But, no worries, with a little science magic you can make your own geodes in a couple of days! Get cracking!

Potassium alum can be found in the spice section of some grocery stores.

TOP TIP

2 days

WHAT YOU NEED

- ☐ raw egg
- ☐ glass
- ☐ warm water
- ☐ paper towel
- ☐ PVA glue (white glue)
- ☐ paintbrush
- ☐ plate
- ☐ measuring spoon
- ☐ 1 cup (150 g) potassium alum powder (a type of salt)
- ☐ small heat-resistant jar
- ☐ spoon
- ☐ 15 drops food coloring

1 Crack an egg carefully into two halves. Clean the inside of the empty eggshell with warm water to remove the membrane. Dry the shell with paper towel. Keep one half shell for "HACK IT!!"

2 Drop a blob of PVA glue into the shell. Use the paintbrush to cover the inside of the shell with a thin, even layer of glue, and just over the edge of the shell as well.

3 While the glue is still wet, pour a tablespoon of alum powder into the eggshell. Do this over the plate. Then gently shake, to cover the inside of the shell with the powder. Pour out and discard the excess powder. Leave the shell to dry overnight.

THE SCIENCE STUFF

CLEAR AS CRYSTAL

The tiny potassium alum crystals dissolve in the hot water. As the water cools slowly and evaporates, the crystals are forced to become solid again. As the crystals become solid they attach themselves to the PVA glue in the eggshells, and with time they grow larger and larger.

4 Ask an adult to help you put ½ cup (75 g) of alum powder into a jar of hot water. Use a spoon to mix until the alum has dissolved. Then mix in 15 drops of food coloring.

5 Use the spoon to push the shell down to the bottom of the jar so it is totally submerged. Leave for two days.

NOW HACK IT!!

★ TRY THIS!

Try adding different solids to the water instead of the potassium alum powder, such as sugar, sea salt, or baking soda. How do your results compare with the alum crystals? Try different food colorings. Some colors work better than others.

★ NOW TRY THIS!

You can make edible crystals too. Ask an adult to help you dissolve 5 cups (750 g) of granulated sugar in 2 cups (475 ml) of boiling water. When the water is cool, add food coloring. Dip a lollipop stick in water and then roll it in sugar. Put the sugar-coated stick in the sugar and water mixture for a week. Yum!

SALT-DRIP STALACTITE

Stalactites are long formations that grow down from cave ceilings and can take millions of years to drip and grow. You, however, can make your own salt-drip stalactite in a few days! Fill two jars with hot water and add 10 drops of food coloring to each. Dissolve 2 tablespoons of salt in each and stir. Dangle the ends of a length of string into each jar, making sure the string hangs down in a "V" between them. Put a little dish underneath the string to collect the drips.

3 days

WHAT YOU NEED

- ☐ 2 cups
- ☐ 4 tbsp salt
- ☐ spoon
- ☐ 20 drops food coloring
- ☐ string

If the weather is warm and the string dries out, use a dropper to wet the string again with salty water.

TOP TIP

In winter, icicles grow when water droplets reach the end of the icicle and quickly freeze, making them longer and longer.

THE SCIENCE STUFF

CRYSTAL GROWTH...

Water containing the dissolved salt moves through the porous string. As the water evaporates, the salt crystals are left behind. The crystal formation keeps growing downward below the string as the drips continue to move down the "stalactite."

The water moves up and along the string very quickly and forms a drip at the "V."

SUPER BLAST!

In limestone caves, ground water saturated with minerals moves through the walls. The water evaporates. Minerals in the water accumulate over time to grow the formations called stalactites.

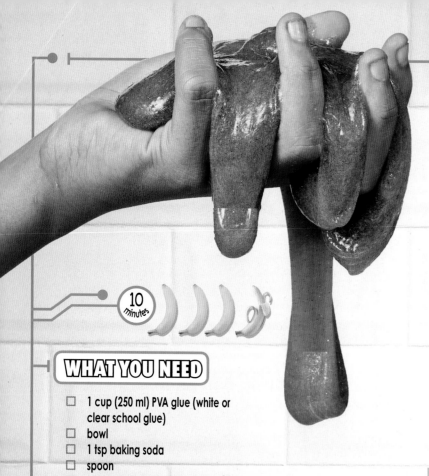

SLIME SCIENCE

Gooey, stringy, slimy, lumpy, snotty —slime is wads of fun! Slime is also easy to make. All you need are some common household items. Time to get extremely sticky!

10 minutes

WHAT YOU NEED

- ☐ 1 cup (250 ml) PVA glue (white or clear school glue)
- ☐ bowl
- ☐ 1 tsp baking soda
- ☐ spoon
- ☐ 10 drops food coloring (optional)
- ☐ glitter (optional)
- ☐ contact lens solution

1 Pour the glue into a bowl.

2 Add the baking soda into the glue and 10 drops of food coloring and/or glitter—it's up to you. Stir it up well.

3 Squeeze in the contact lens solution a little at a time, mixing it well as you go. Remember! Do NOT squirt too much all at once.

GOING GOOEY...

Glue is a polymer—it's made of long chains of molecules, like really, really tiny strings. The contact lens solution causes the chains to be linked together—so they get tangled up and stay like that.

Watch it! Adding too much liquid will make the slime runny.

TOP TIP

4 Keep squirting in the contact lens solution until the mixture comes away easily from the side of the bowl and is solid enough for you to hold.

Green food coloring and glitter make great dragon snot slime!

NOW HACK IT!!

⭐ TRY THIS!

For fluffy slime, add a good squirt of shaving foam before mixing in the contact lens solution.

⭐ NOW TRY THIS!

Make small amounts of different-colored slime and then mix them together for rainbow slime!

SOLID/LIQUID GOO!

Most substances are either a solid or a liquid. Right? Wrong! Some strange mixtures can be either. Depending whether you push, pull, squeeze, or pour it, this substance, known as oobleck, acts as either a solid or a liquid. Mixtures like this are known as non-Newtonian fluids and are super-fun to play with.

WHAT YOU NEED

⏱ 10 minutes

- ☒ large bowl
- ☒ 1 cup (240 ml) water
- ☒ 2 cups (220 g) cornstarch
- ☒ wooden spoon
- ☒ food coloring (optional)

1 Pour the water into the bowl. Add the cornstarch—a little at a time. Stir with the spoon as you go along.

2 Keep stirring until the mixture has a gooey consistency. Add the food coloring if you are using it.

46

THE SCIENCE STUFF

NON-NEWTONIAN GOO...

Cornstarch is a natural polymer and behaves like the glue in the slime on page 44. When mixed with water the polymers make a special kind of slime. As you squeeze the oobleck, you are applying pressure. Pressure is a force and it makes the blob act more like a solid. The more tangled the polymer strands get the less they can move. When you relax your hand and use less force, the blob flows like a liquid!

Don't pour the goo down the drain. It may dry out and block it!

TOP TIP

3 If you find it difficult to stir the mixture (you might), you may want to use your hands at this point.

4 Grab a handful and let it ooze through your fingers. Now roll it into a hard ball and keep moving it from one hand to the other. Does it feel different when it is relaxed or squeezed?

NOW HACK IT!!

⭐ TRY IT!

What happens if you use more water? Does the mixture eventually stop going solid? Can you think of some practical uses for non-Newtonian fluids?

⭐ NOW TRY THIS!

Make cornstarch stretchy slime by swapping the water for dish soap. Add a bit of dish soap at a time, until the mixture comes away from the bowl and you can lift it out. Keep squeezing the mixture and it will become stretchy slime!

OOBLECK

15 minutes

Now take the oobleck a bit further and make lots and lots and lots! Fill a whole dish with oobleck! Challenge a friend to stand on it without sinking in and without making a mess of their feet. Once they are on it, can they lift their feet up and step around it? What happens if they wiggle their toes?

You might want to help your friend onto the oobleck!

TOP TIP

THE SCIENCE STUFF

WALK ON LIQUID!
Just like when you squeeze the oobleck, standing on it causes the water molecules to become rigid, trapped between the starch chains. It feels like standing on a tiled floor! Wiggle your toes however, and the molecules can move again and your feet will sink!

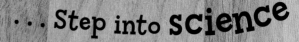
. . . Step into science

¾ Pint

NOW
HACK IT!!

★ **TRY THIS!**
What happens if you put other objects in the dish full of oobleck? Try something light, like a coin, and compare it to something heavier, like a marble. Which sinks faster?

There should be some super slurping noises when your friend steps off!

... careful when you step off!

SHAKE IT UP ICE CREAM!

It's hard to believe you can make ice cream in just 20 minutes, but you can, and it tastes great too! And you don't even need a freezer. The magic ingredient is salt. Sounds impossible? Give it a try!

WHAT YOU NEED

30 minutes

- [ ] small sealable plastic bag
- [ ] ½ cup (125 ml) whole milk
- [ ] 1 tbsp sugar
- [ ] ½ tsp vanilla extract
- [ ] large sealable plastic bag
- [ ] large plastic container with lid (gallon size works well!)
- [ ] 4 cups of ice
- [ ] 6 tbsp rock salt

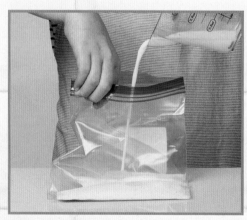

1 Pour the milk, sugar, and vanilla extract into the smaller bag. Shut it tightly, pushing out as much air as possible.

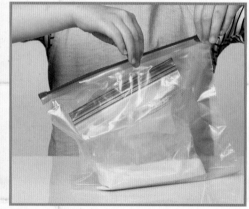

2 Place the bag into the larger bag. Seal securely, again pushing out as much air as you can.

THE SCIENCE STUFF

SALT IS COOL

The secret to making ice cream is to lower the melting point of ice. Just add salt! Adding salt lowers the temperature at which water will melt or freeze. When ice melts it has to take the heat energy from somewhere—in this case it takes it from the milk mixture, causing the milk to freeze instead.

Wear gloves or hold towels when you shake. It's cold!

TOP TIP

NOW HACK IT!!

⭐ ### TRY THIS!

Can you make ice cream if you add fruit? Mash some berries and add them to your mixture. Does it still freeze? What happens if you use yogurt instead of milk?

⭐ ### NOW TRY THIS!

Pop your ice cream into a cone, cover it with chocolate and sprinkles, and eat! Yum!

3 Put the ice into the container and add the salt. Put the lid on the container and shake well for five minutes so that the ice is covered in salt.

4 Take the bags containing the ice-cream mix and put in the middle of the ice. Shake the container for 15 minutes. Take the bags out and you will have ice cream!

PLANT REACTIONS

Living organisms like plants and animals (including humans) have chemical reactions taking place in and around them every day. For example, when we eat, chemicals called enzymes break down the food so we can absorb the chemicals that we need to grow healthy and strong. Plants make their own food through a process called photosynthesis. This uses energy from light, which helps carbon dioxide from the air to react with water to form glucose (a sugar) and oxygen. Find out how they do this through these planty experiments and discover what happens if one of those growing elements goes missing!

THE FOOD CHAIN...

Photosynthesis is one of the most important reactions on Earth because it takes carbon dioxide gas out of the air and turns it into glucose, which is the source of all molecules in all living organisms (that's why plants are always at the bottom of food chains). Without photosynthesis, there would be no plants, so there would be no food for any animals!

FLOWER POWER

Think flowers stay the same color? Think again! Change the color of white flowers and find out how plants suck water up from the ground.

Watch out, this chapter can get muddy!

54

MAKING MOLECULES...

Plants take carbon dioxide gas from the air and water from the soil. Chlorophyll is a green pigment that makes plants green. Chlorophyll absorbs light and uses this light energy to cause carbon dioxide and water to react with each other. This reaction makes glucose and oxygen gas. This glucose is then used to make all the molecules a plant needs to grow. (And then animals eat plants, so they can use the molecules in the plants to make their own molecules).

SOW THE SEEDS

Find out what a plant needs to grow by conducting the cress experiment, the germination jar, and the bean maze. If you are patient enough you can eat your experiment too!

JUNGLE TIME

Make your own jungle in a jar! It's a whole ecosystem on your windowsill, complete with clouds and rain!

CRESS TEST

Plant seeds need very basic things in order to start growing. Let's grow some plants to see what it takes to get a garden started! Pop cotton balls into three egg shells. Find objects like egg cups to keep them standing up. Sprinkle the cotton balls with cress seeds. Put one on a sunny windowsill and water daily. Place one on a sunny windowsill, but do NOT water it. Place one in a box in a dark cupboard. Water the pot daily—in the dark! Watch what happens over 5 days. Compare how the plants grow!

WHAT YOU NEED

5 days

- ☐ 3 clean eggshells (or small pots)
- ☐ garden cress seeds
- ☐ cotton balls
- ☐ water
- ☐ box

The seeds that are denied light often grow super quickly because they are desperately looking for light.

One grows **yellow**. One grows **green**...

Cress seeds don't need soil to grow. They hold all the nutrients (food) they need.

THE SCIENCE STUFF

PLANT POWER...

The seeds need water to begin to grow (germinate), so the seeds without water will never get growing. The seeds in the dark that do have water will germinate, but without light they cannot create chlorophyll, which is what makes plants green. If you move these watered seeds out into the light they will then turn green. The seedlings grown in the light from the beginning can absorb light and therefore make chlorophyll, so they are green right from the start.

It's a no show with no water.

With water and light you get a perfect head of cress hair.

...one grows **nothing** at all!

GERMINATION JAR

All plants need food to survive. But instead of going to the dining room or kitchen to find food, plants can eat without moving at all! Plants take in carbon dioxide from the air, they suck water through their roots, and absorb energy from the sun. Watch a plant start to grow, or germinate, by planting a bean in a glass jar. How quickly can you grow more beans?

WHAT YOU NEED

2-3 days

- ☐ 1 sheet of paper towel
- ☐ clear jar
- ☐ bean seed
- ☐ water

Don't overwater the bean or it might go moldy.

TOP TIP

Runner beans or broad beans work well for this experiment.

1 Wrap a piece of paper towel around the inside edge of a jar. Insert the bean between the paper towel and the wall of the jar.

2 Pour a little water into the bottom of the jar to moisten the paper towel. Then put the jar in a sunny place. Make sure the paper towel is kept damp.

3 The first part to grow is called a radicle and it always grows downward. The radicle will become a root. This process is called germination.

THE SCIENCE STUFF

LIGHT AND GROWTH...

When plants use energy from light for photosynthesis they make glucose and oxygen. They use the glucose to make other molecules they need so that they can make cells, which are the building blocks of living things. A plant has lots of different types of cells, which each do a particular job. Some cells make leaves—these cells are packed with chlorophyll to absorb lots of light. Other types of cells make the roots—these cells have a really big surface area so that they can absorb lots of water.

The bean holds enough food for the seed to germinate and make a shoot that reaches the light.

4 After a few days a shoot and green leaves will appear. The leaves search for light.

5 When the bean has roots and a stalk, plant it outside in soil.

NOW HACK IT!!

⭐ TRY THIS!

Try growing other seeds from foods that you eat. It's best to start most seeds in soil. Try planting the seeds from an avocado, an apple, or even a plum. Can you grow an entire tree?

⭐ NOW TRY THIS!

Try planting sunflower seeds in a jar. Do the flower seeds work as well as the beans? The sunflower seeds will probably grow best if they are put in a pot of soil before placing on your windowsill.

59

BEAN MAZE

You might not be able to find your way around in the dark. But guess what? A plant can! Plants will search for and find even a tiny bit of light. Build a box maze to show how determined plants are in their search for light!

SEE THE LIGHT...

Plants have some special hormones that help them to grow and develop. Auxins are one type of plant hormone. In a shoot, auxin causes cells to get longer. This can help the plant to grow toward the light. Auxin causes the cells on the shaded side to grow and elongate more, so that the whole shoot bends toward the light.

WHAT YOU NEED

☐ plant pot
☐ soil
☐ bean seed
☐ water
☐ shoe box
☐ cardboard
☐ scissors
☐ tape

1 week

TOP TIP

Put the box on a windowsill that gets lots of light. Keep the plant watered.

1 Fill the pot about three quarters full of soil. Plant a bean seed in the center and water the soil well. Leave the seed to germinate. After 3 or 4 days you should see a shoot.

2 Take a shoebox and cut a hole in the side of the box at the top. This is where the light will get in. Paint the inside of the box a dark color.

3 Decorate the outside of the box with some bright paint so that the box will look good on your windowsill.

4 Cut three pieces of cardboard. Fold a flap at the end of each piece and tape inside the box on alternate sides to create a maze. Put the pot in the box and close the lid.

The plant has to search for the light and work its way up through the maze to get to it.

NOW HACK IT!!

TRY THIS!

Set a more challenging maze! This time make a more complicated journey for the plant with more pieces of card or a smaller hole.

NOW TRY THIS!

Try the experiment using artificial light. Do different colored lights affect the way the plant grows?

SUCTION POWER!

Can you master this flower color-changing trick? It's actually really easy and it's the flower that does all the work. Plants need to drink lots of water to grow. They take water through their roots and suck it all the way up to the leaves and petals. Prove that flower stems can suck up water by watching colored water magically dye flower petals!

1 Half fill the vases with water. Remove any leaves from the stems of the flowers.

2 Put 2 or 3 drops of food coloring or ink into two of the vases. Use a different color in each vase. Put a flower into each vase. Keep the vases in a sunny spot.

3 days

WHAT YOU NEED

- ☐ 3 glass vases
- ☐ water
- ☐ 3 white flowers
- ☐ food coloring or ink

White roses, chrysanthemums, and daisies work well!

TOP TIP

THE SCIENCE STUFF

CAPILLARY ACTION ...

Capillary action is the force that takes water upward to the plant's flowers. The water is attracted to the surface of tiny tubes in the flowers' stalks and, coupled with water molecules being attracted to each other, this makes the water rise. So the colored water in the glass moves up the stems and into the flowers and they change color.

3 Leave the flowers undisturbed for three days. Observe the flowers every day and watch how they change over time. Compare the flowers in colored water with the one in uncolored water.

NOW HACK IT!!

★ **TRY THIS!**

Does capillary action work with celery? Cut 2 in (5 cm) off the bottom of a stalk of celery. Put the celery stalk in a glass of colored water with the cut side down. Observe the celery over the next few days. What happens to the veins running up the stalk?

FUN WITH PLANTS!

There's more to plants than meets the eye. You can clone them, extract water from them, and even create plant ecosystems!

SEEDLESS GROWTH

2

You can grow a plant without a seed. Use scissors to cut a straight stem from a plant. Remove the lower leaves from the stem and put the stem into a small glass of water. When roots start to appear plant the stem in a pot with compost. Water well and cover the plant with a plastic bag to keep it humid. Put the pot in a warm, sunny place. You will soon have an identical baby plant!

WHO KNEW?

Some plants can make identical copies of themselves by producing runners, tubers, or plantlets. Gardeners also grow new plants by taking cuttings.

GARLIC FROM GARLIC

1

Place a clove of unpeeled garlic in a short glass. Then pour in just enough water to cover the bottom of the glass. Put the glass on a sunny window ledge. When the leaves are about 2 inches (5 cm) tall, trim them and sprinkle over your food!

WHO KNEW?

There's more to garlic than just the bulb! The bulb is food storage for the plant. If you water a clove, there is enough food inside to grow stems. Trim the stems and they taste just like a garlic clove!

LEAF DROPLETS

Prove that trees suck up water through their roots and expel it out of their leaves by doing this experiment. On a sunny day, tie a plastic bag around a leafy branch with a small stone inside it to weigh it down. After 24 hours see how much water has collected in the bag.

WHO KNEW?

All plants carry water from the roots up through the stems and then "sweat" it out through the leaves. This is called transpiration. It helps to cool the plant as well as transport nutrients through it.

JUNGLE IN A JAR

Put some stones in the bottom of a large jar with a lid. Then add a layer of soil. Plant a small plant in the soil and water it well. Seal the jar making sure the top is on tight so that no air can get in or out. What happens to it over a week?

WHO KNEW?

The water is sucked up through the roots and transpires out of the leaves. This moisture forms little "clouds" in the jar and the water drops down the sides into the soil again. It keeps going, just like a real jungle with its own ecosystem. . . and your plant will thrive!

RULES

FORCES AND PRESSURE

Science is all around us. It's happening everywhere, but often we are too busy to notice it. Scientists ask questions. Why does that boat float? Why does water form droplets? Why doesn't oil mix with water? How can I use science to play tricks on my friends to make them soaking wet? (See page 76.) All these questions, and more, are answered in this section.

FEEL THE FORCE...

A force is a push or a pull and causes a change in speed, direction or shape. Forces never exist on their own, they act in pairs. For example, when you stand on the floor, the weight of your body is pushing down on the ground and it is pushing back up on your body. This stops you sinking into the ground! In the same way when something is falling from the sky, its weight is pulling it down and the air pushes back against the object slowing down its fall.

If a force is concentrated into a small point it creates a very big pressure, but if the force is spread over a bigger area then the pressure is lower. For example, if someone who is wearing stiletto heels stands on your toe it will be much more painful than if the same person stands on your toe when wearing flat shoes.

PICK AND MIX

Create beautiful lava lamps while learning why oil and water don't mix.

Watch out, this chapter can get messsy!

TOP TIP

DENSITY DOES IT
Find out what density means and build an impossible density tower using different liquids...then drop your toys in to see if they float!

EGG-STRAORDINARY
There is no way this egg won't smash even if it's attached to a parachute. . . Wrong! Try it and see!

A PINCH OF SALT
Discover why you float more easily in the sea than you do in a swimming pool!

PACKED PARTICLES...
The density of a material or object depends on the number of particles packed into a certain volume (or space). When there are lots of particles packed very close together then the material is described as being very dense. It's a bit like a room that is packed full of lots and lots of people who are all squished together. If the particles in a material are not so tightly packed then the material is described as being less dense.

69

AN EGG-SPERIMENT

We all know what would happen if you tried to stand on an egg, right? SPLAT! But eggs are tougher than you think. Try this! Fill a tray of eggs, making sure that you have the pointy sides facing up. Ask a friend to help you stand on them carefully. Make sure you spread your feet over lots of the eggs as you step on or you'll have scrambled eggs!

WHAT YOU NEED

5 minutes

- ☐ **1 large egg tray (or 2 small trays)**
- ☐ **eggs**

Remove your shoes and socks before you step on—just in case!

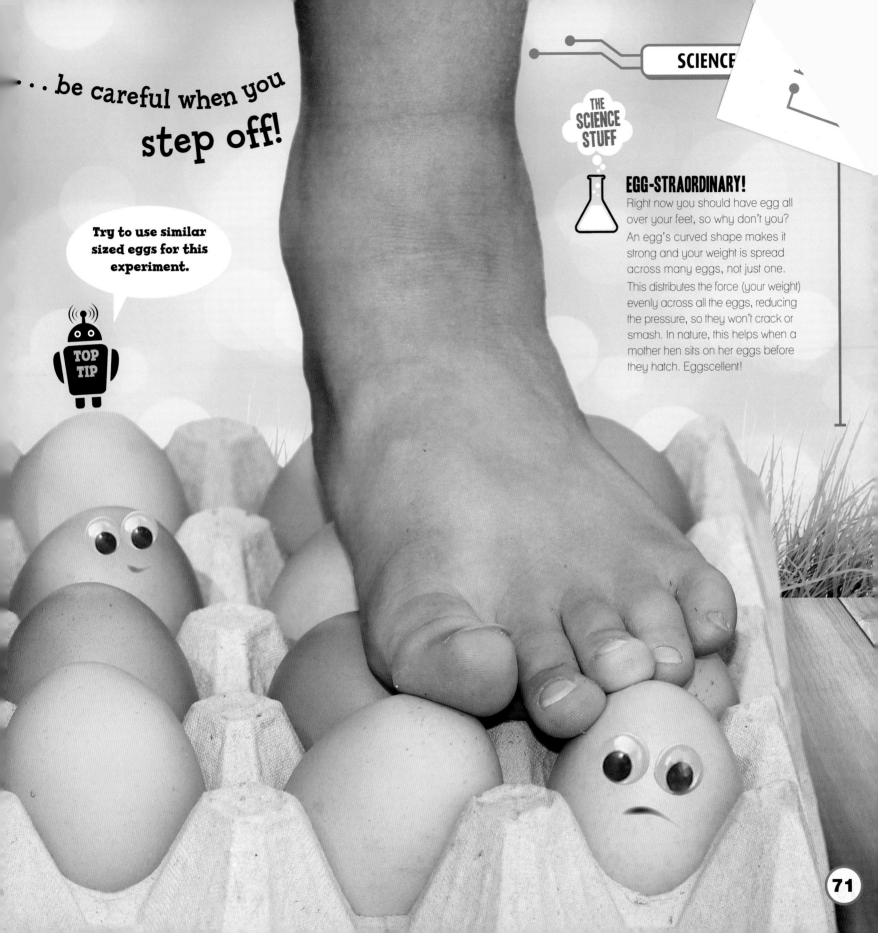

...be careful when you **step off!**

Try to use similar sized eggs for this experiment.

TOP TIP

THE SCIENCE STUFF

EGG-STRAORDINARY!

Right now you should have egg all over your feet, so why don't you? An egg's curved shape makes it strong and your weight is spread across many eggs, not just one. This distributes the force (your weight) evenly across all the eggs, reducing the pressure, so they won't crack or smash. In nature, this helps when a mother hen sits on her eggs before they hatch. Eggscellent!

SINK OR FLOAT?

It seems crazy that a marble sinks in water, but HUGE boats can float. It's actually not all about weight. Build your own boat and find out why!

WHAT YOU NEED

15 minutes

- ☐ large bowl of water
- ☐ modeling clay
- ☐ marbles
- ☐ paper, toothpick, tape to make sail (optional)

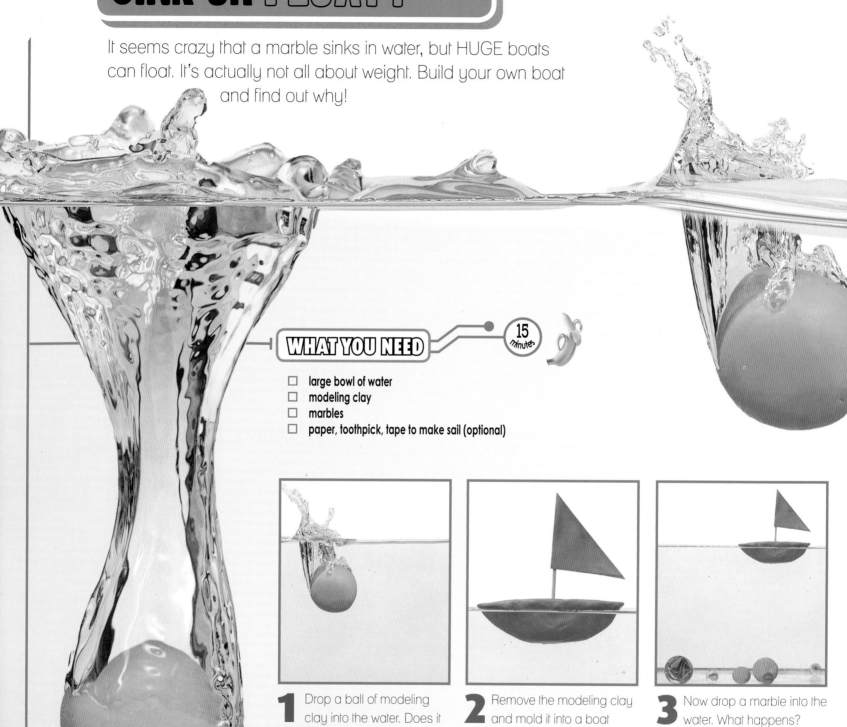

1 Drop a ball of modeling clay into the water. Does it sink or float?

2 Remove the modeling clay and mold it into a boat shape. Add a toothpick sail if you have made one. Does the boat float?

3 Now drop a marble into the water. What happens? How can you make it float?

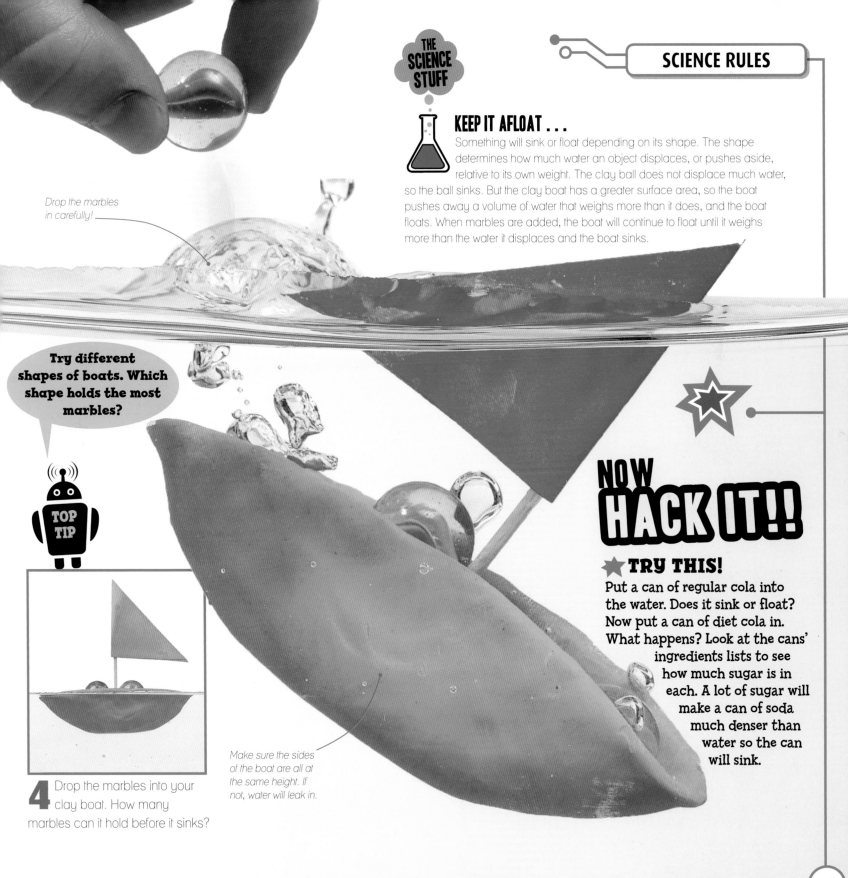

THE SCIENCE STUFF

KEEP IT AFLOAT . . .

Something will sink or float depending on its shape. The shape determines how much water an object displaces, or pushes aside, relative to its own weight. The clay ball does not displace much water, so the ball sinks. But the clay boat has a greater surface area, so the boat pushes away a volume of water that weighs more than it does, and the boat floats. When marbles are added, the boat will continue to float until it weighs more than the water it displaces and the boat sinks.

Drop the marbles in carefully!

Try different shapes of boats. Which shape holds the most marbles?

TOP TIP

Make sure the sides of the boat are all at the same height. If not, water will leak in.

4 Drop the marbles into your clay boat. How many marbles can it hold before it sinks?

NOW HACK IT!!

⭐ TRY THIS!

Put a can of regular cola into the water. Does it sink or float? Now put a can of diet cola in. What happens? Look at the cans' ingredients lists to see how much sugar is in each. A lot of sugar will make a can of soda much denser than water so the can will sink.

HOW MANY DROPS?

5 minutes

- ☐ coin
- ☐ water
- ☐ syringe or eye dropper
- ☐ a steady hand!

How many water drops can you balance on a coin? More than you think! Clean a coin with water—don't use any soap—and dry it. Fill a dropper with water and slowly drop a drop onto the coin. Keep your hand steady. How many drops can fit? You'll be surprised how many the coin can hold!

PENNY TENSION...

Water is made up of lots of tiny molecules. The molecules attract, or stick to, one another. The water molecules at the surface don't have anything to stick to above them, only below and to the side of them. This unbalance creates a thin skin on the surface of the water. This is called surface tension. Surface tension is the reason why small insects can "walk" on water!

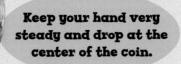

Keep your hand very steady and drop at the center of the coin.

TOP TIP

NOW HACK IT!!

★ TRY THIS!

Soap separates the water molecules and decreases surface tension. Try adding a little soap to the water. How many drops of water can you fit on the coin now?

★ NOW TRY THIS!

Do other liquids have surface tension too? Try dropping vinegar, oil, soda, or salt water. Count how many drops the coin can hold.

THE AMAZING BOTTLE TRICK

This is a clever trick if you want to get someone wet! All you need is a big plastic bottle and a pin. Simply fill a bottle about ¾ full with water and screw on the cap tightly. Then take a thumbtack and puncture about 12 holes just above the bottom. Ask an adult to help you with this. As you do it, some water might leak out, but when you let go you won't be able to tell the holes are there. Now all you have to do is get someone to either pick the bottle up or unscrew the lid. Shower time!

Ask someone to pass you the bottle!

TOP TIP

DRINK ME!

WHAT YOU NEED 15 minutes

- ☐ large empty soda bottle
- ☐ thumbtack

1 Evenly space the holes around the bottom of the bottle full of water.

See how many holes you can puncture in the bottle. What happens if you position them higher up?

THE SCIENCE STUFF

SQUEEZE, ARRGGHH!

An empty bottle is full of air. When you fill it with water the air molecules escape out of the top. When you tilt the bottle to pour, air rushes in letting the water fall out. When you do the experiment and make the tiny holes in the bottle, the holes are not big enough to let the air in. The water molecules also work together to seal the holes—surface tension. Squeezing the bottle forces the water out. When you release the cap, the air rushes in, pushing the water out of the holes.

DENSITY TOWER

Create your own colorful density tower, and discover if some liquids can sit on top of other liquids. Then drop in all sorts of different objects. Can you predict what sinks, what floats, and what just hangs around the different layers?

THE SCIENCE STUFF

DENSE OR NOT...

The clue is in the heading, it's all about density! A liquid's density is the amount of mass in a given unit. The same amount of different liquids can have different densities. The densest liquid (the honey) will sink to the bottom, while the least dense liquid (the oil) floats to the top. Different objects have different densities too. A ping-pong ball may be bigger than a marble, but it is full of air, so it is less dense and sits on the top.

Wash the dropper well each time you use it.

TOP TIP

WHAT YOU NEED

10 minutes

- ☐ glass or jar
- ☐ 2 tbsp honey
- ☐ syringe or eye dropper
- ☐ 2 tbsp dish soap
- ☐ food coloring
- ☐ water
- ☐ dish

- ☐ 2 tbsp vegetable oil
- ☐ metal screw
- ☐ grape

- ☐ marble
- ☐ bouncy ball
- ☐ ping-pong ball

1 Pour the honey into the glass. Make sure you don't get any on the sides of the glass.

2 Use the dropper to add in the dish soap. Be careful with this layer. It is best to hold the dropper right at the side of the glass. Then squeeze to drip the liquid down the side.

3 Add a few drops of food coloring to the water in a separate dish. Use the dropper to add the colored water layer to the glass. Again, hold the dropper to the side and let it dribble down.

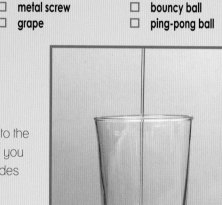

NOW HACK IT!!

★ TRY THIS!

Make a tower with other liquids, like milk or ketchup. Then try dropping different objects in. Does a tomato, a raisin, or a paperclip sink or float?

★ NOW TRY THIS!

Fill three glasses with warm water. Dissolve 1 tsp of salt in one, 1 tsp of sugar in another, and leave one as it is. Drop a raisin into each glass. Do the raisins sink or float? Do you think sugar or salt makes water more or less dense?

4 The last layer is the vegetable oil. Use the dropper to add the oil. Now you should have a perfect density tower!

5 Next it's time to test the layers. Drop the items in one by one. See where they all wind up. Why do you think some sink and others float?

1 Pour the water into the container. Add the vegetable oil. Does the oil mix with the water?

LAVA LAMP

Have you ever noticed a rainbow of oil floating on top of a puddle, or tried to clean a greasy plate with just water? Oil and water just don't seem to get on. Discover why this is . . . and make a lava lamp while you find out!

WHAT YOU NEED

10 minutes

- ☐ clean, clear container with lid
- ☐ 1 cup (250 ml) water
- ☐ ½ cup (125 ml) vegetable oil
- ☐ small dish
- ☐ 2 tbsp dish soap
- ☐ 5 drops food coloring
- ☐ syringe or eye dropper

2 Use the lid to tightly close the container. Now shake it. Do the oil and water mix now? Leave to settle and watch what happens.

3 Mix the dish soap with the food coloring in the small dish.

4 Using a syringe or dropper, squirt some of the colored dish soap into the container. Squirt lots more and leave to settle.

THE SCIENCE STUFF

MIX AND MATCH...

Oil molecules and water molecules are not attracted to each other—they don't mix. Oil has a lower density than water so it always floats on top of it. Dish soap, however, is attracted to both water and oil molecules. It grabs onto both and moves through them.

IN THE REAL WORLD...

Water doesn't clean grease (oil) off dirty dishes. But dish soap attracts the grease and pulls it towards the water. Clean dishes!

NOW HACK IT!!

TRY THIS!
Pour a teaspoon of salt into the mixture, after step 4. What happens?

NOW TRY THIS
Add ¾ cup (200 ml) of water to a 2-pint (1-liter) bottle. Using a jug or funnel, fill the bottle with vegetable oil. Add 10 drops of food coloring and then half a seltzer or fizzy vitamin tablet. Watch the colored fizz!

HACK IT SOME MORE!
What happens if you add a raw egg, vinegar, or another food coloring?

SALT SEPARATION!

Suppose you are presented with two glasses of water. One glass is filled with salty seawater. The other contains tap water. Can you pick out which one is which—without tasting them? You can with this experiment! Warning! You will need a steady hand, and be careful, this experiment can get you very wet!

You may want to conduct this experiment over a sink!

WHAT YOU NEED **20** minutes

- ☐ 2 identical drinking glasses
- ☐ tap water
- ☐ 1 tsp food coloring
- ☐ 1 tbsp table salt
- ☐ stirrer or spoon
- ☐ scissors
- ☐ cardboard

TOP TIP

1 Fill the glasses to the rim with water.

2 Drop the food coloring into one of the glasses.

3 Put the salt into the other glass of water. Stir to mix well. Make sure both glasses are completely full of water. If not, add some.

4 Cut a piece of cardboard that is bigger than the glasses' rim and place it on top of the colored-water glass.

THE SCIENCE STUFF

LIQUID LAYERS...

Both glasses started out with the same amount of water in them. When salt is added to water there are more particles in the same amount of space making the salt water more dense. The mixture of food coloring and tap water is less dense than the salty water. So the colored water floats on top, just like oil does on water.

THE DEAD SEA

The Dead Sea is a giant lake that is one of the world's saltiest bodies of water. Because the water is so dense, you can float without moving your arms and legs. You can read a newspaper while you float!

The colored water mixture stops where the salt mixture begins.

NOW HACK IT!!

⭐ TRY IT!

What happens if you just pour some colored water onto some salt water in a glass? Does it sit on top or does it mix in?

⭐ NOW TRY THIS!

Now try the same experiment using 1 tbsp of sugar instead of salt. Do you think sugar water is denser than salt water?

5 Lift the glass with one hand. Hold the cardboard down with your other hand. Flip the glass upside down. Don't let go of the cardboard!

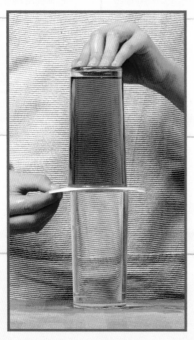

6 Lower the colored water glass onto the salt water glass. Keep the glass rims exactly together and gently slide the card out. Does the colored water sink?

Why doesn't the **green water** mix into the **salt water?**

BAG OF TRICKS

How do you puncture a hole (or lots of holes) in a bag filled with water without getting wet? Sound impossible? Try it! It might be best to do this project over a sink or a bathtub, or even outside if it's a sunny day, just in case things don't go quite according to plan. After all, that's what experimenting is all about!

WHAT YOU NEED

5 minutes

- ☐ water
- ☐ small sealable plastic bag
- ☐ several super-sharp pencils

Hold the top firmly. You don't want to drop the bag!

1 Fill the bag with water and seal it shut. Take a pencil and confidently stab the bag. Push it all the way through and out the other side. Are you wet?

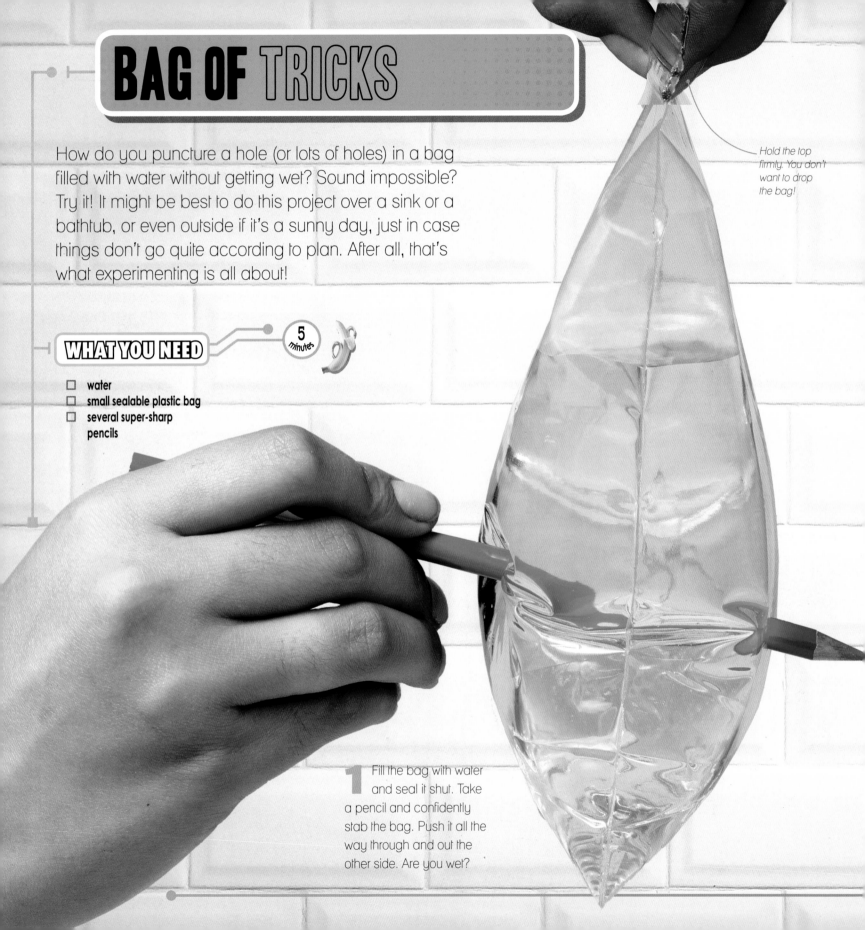

THE SCIENCE STUFF

NO-LEAK BAG...

Slime and plastic bags have something in common. They are both made of polymers. (You learned about polymers on page 44.) As the pencil pushes through, it slips between the polymer molecules, which are formed as long, flexible strands. These strands squeeze back against the pencil sealing the hole around it. And the water stays in! When you pull the pencils out the molecules remain where they were pushed and the water leaks out.

NOW HACK IT!!

★ TRY THIS!

Balloons are made of polymers too. Let's see if you can pierce through one! First, blow up a balloon. Then let out about one third of the air and tie a knot at the end. Take a bamboo skewer and coat it with vegetable oil. Push the skewer into the end of the balloon near the knot. Now, see if you can push the skewer all the way through the other end of the balloon without popping it.

2 Keep going with the pencils, but don't make the holes too close to one another. Try to keep the pencils from touching. How many can you stab through?

Make sure the pencils go through the part of the bag that contains water.

TOP TIP

FUN with WATER

1

ICE PICK UP

Can you pick up an ice cube with a piece of string? Yes you can. Here's how! Simply add a layer of salt to the surface of the ice and lay the string on top. Wait a minute. Then pick up the string. The ice is attached to the string!

WHO KNEW?

As seen on page 51, the salt lowers the freezing point of water. That's why adding salt to the ice cube causes water to come out. The string absorbs some of the melted liquid. Since the ice is still chilly, it refreezes the melted water, including the water in the string. That's how the string gets stuck.

Water is just water, right? Actually water in science is far more surprising than you think. You can fiddle with its freezing point, perform tricks with it, and decorate paper with it. Watch out, you may get wet!

2

SUPER COOL FIZZ

Put a small bottle of sparkling water into the freezer for two hours. Take it out, give it to a friend and ask them to open it. As they open it, it will freeze before their eyes!

WHO KNEW?

Carbonated water contains carbon dioxide (CO_2) and naturally-occurring salts. These cause it to have a lower freezing point than water. That means it can go below the normal freezing point before it freezes. When it is opened, the CO_2 rushes out causing the freezing point to rise and the water instantly freezes!

3 WEIRD WATER

Take a glass or jar, making sure a playing card can fit over the rim. Fill the glass with water all the way to the top. Stand over a sink and hold the card on top then turn the glass upside-down, keeping your hand on the card. Now the tricky bit! Take your hand away from the card and it should stay in place. Are you brave enough to try it?

WHO KNEW?

It is air pressure that holds the card in place. Air is all around us and it pushes in different directions, up as well as down. The air pushing up on the card is strong enough to stop the water from pushing down. So the higher pressure outside pushes against the card and holds it in place.

4 MARBLE PAPER MARVEL

Fill a large shallow dish with water. Time to mix "paint." Put a tablespoon of vegetable oil into each of four dishes. Then put a different food coloring into each dish. Drop the mixtures onto the water. Place a piece of paper over the paint. Carefully lift the sheet and set it aside to dry. You have marbled paper!

WHO KNEW?

As you have seen on page 80, oil and water don't mix. The water-based food coloring won't stick to the paper where there are oil bubbles, and this creates the marbling effect.

FLYING PING-PONG BALLS

Put some ping-pong balls under pressure. Air pressure that is. Turn a hairdryer to the cool setting and turn it on. Hold a ping-pong ball above the blast of air and let go. Does the ping-pong ball float above the hairdryer?

15 minutes

WHAT YOU NEED

☐ ping-pong balls
☐ hairdryer

TOP TIP

Ask an adult to help you with the hairdryer.

Try adding more **balls** on *top*.

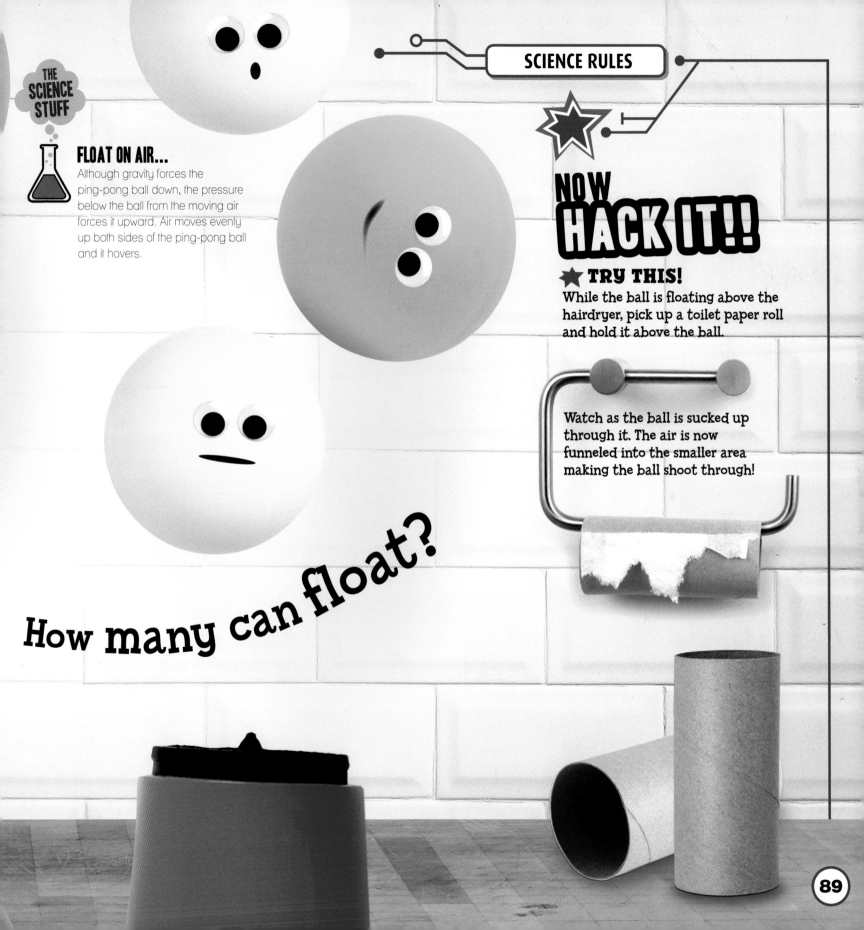

THE SCIENCE STUFF

FLOAT ON AIR...
Although gravity forces the ping-pong ball down, the pressure below the ball from the moving air forces it upward. Air moves evenly up both sides of the ping-pong ball and it hovers.

NOW HACK IT!!

★ TRY THIS!
While the ball is floating above the hairdryer, pick up a toilet paper roll and hold it above the ball.

Watch as the ball is sucked up through it. The air is now funneled into the smaller area making the ball shoot through!

How many can float?

CAN YOU MAKE AN EGG FLY?

Drop a raw egg from a high window. What happens? SPLAT! So can you think of a way to make an egg land without breaking? How about making a parachute for an egg? Let's see if that will result in a safe landing!

Make sure you hold the parachute strings straight as you drop.

 **WHAT YOU NEED**

 **20 minutes**

- ☐ thick, plastic trash bag
- ☐ scissors
- ☐ ruler
- ☐ hole punch
- ☐ ball of string
- ☐ sealable plastic bag x 2
- ☐ raw egg

 **TOP TIP**

1 Use a ruler to measure a piece of trash bag, about 20 x 20 in (50 x 50 cm). Cut the square out.

2 Punch a hole in each corner of the square. Make sure the hole is not too close to the edge.

3 Measure and cut four pieces of string, each 20 in (50 cm) long. Tie one to each corner of the square.

4 Put the egg into the sealable bag. Then tightly zip close the bag.

5 Gather the four ends of the string. Use them to make a knot around the bag. Tie tightly! The bag needs to be securely attached to the strings.

NOW HACK IT!!

Make sure each string is tied tightly!

⭐ **TRY THIS!**
Time how long it takes for the egg to reach the ground. What happens if you use longer strings? Does a bigger parachute float more slowly?

⭐ **NOW TRY THIS!**
What happens if you use a different parachute material, such as fabric?

THE SCIENCE STUFF

6 Ask an adult to help you drop the parachute out of a second floor window. Does the egg break when it lands?

FLOATING EGG...

When the egg is dropped, the strings pull and the parachute opens up. The egg drops due to gravity, but the the large surface area of the parachute traps a lot of air molecules. These air molecules push against the underside of the parachute, slowing it down. As a result the parachute and the egg will—hopefully!—fall gently to the ground.

RUBBER-BAND CANNON

Challenge your friends to make a launcher using a potato chip tube and a soda bottle. You will need some light balls to launch and a row of empty plastic bottles or soda cans to aim at. Remember never to aim at people, or pets, or objects other than your targets.

THE SCIENCE STUFF

ENERGY SHIFT...
The launcher is a simple device that stores and transfers energy. When you pull the bottle back and stretch the rubber bands, kinetic (movement) energy from your hand is stored as elastic energy in the rubber bands. When you let go, the stored elastic energy is transferred to the foil ball. The ball gains kinetic energy. The distance the ball travels depends on its mass, kinetic energy, and the angle at which it is launched.

30 minutes

WHAT YOU NEED

- ☐ sturdy cardboard tube (a potato chips container works)
- ☐ scissors
- ☐ ruler
- ☐ 2 rubber bands
- ☐ tape
- ☐ small soda bottle
- ☐ pencil
- ☐ aluminum foil

1 Ask an adult to help you cut out the bottom of the tube. Cut two 2-in (5-cm) slits each side, ½ an inch (1 cm) apart. See picture below to help you.

2 Hook a rubber band over each pair of slits. Then secure the top with tape.

3 Ask an adult to make two holes in either side of the bottle, near the neck. Push a pencil through the holes.

Make sure the elastic bands are thick enough to stretch far.

TOP TIP

NOW HACK IT!!

★ TRY THIS!

Try making bigger or smaller foil balls. Which travels the farthest? Now try some other balls. Does the mass of the balls affect how far they go? Does pulling the bands back a long or a short way affect how far the balls go?

4 Drop the bottle into the tube with the top poking out. Hook the elastic bands over each end of the pencil.

5 Now the cannon is ready to fire. Squeeze some foil into a ball. Pop it into the bottom of your cannon, pull the bottle back, and let go!

Wrap elastic bands around the foil ball to make it bigger and heavier.

SUPER-CHARGED

ENERGY AND MAGNETISM

Get ready for the buzzing section of the book! It's all about electricity and magnetism—those invisible forces that are all around us and part of our lives every day. In order to learn about electricity and magnetism, get out there and make your own! From creating static electricity and your own magnets, to making circuits that light a bulb using fruit, this super-charged section is going to make your hair stand on end!

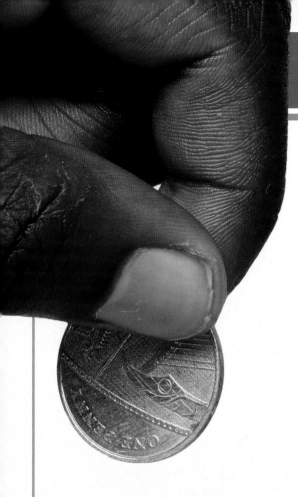

I'VE GOT THE POWER

Create a coin tower battery that not only lights an LED bulb, but make a tall one and it could power your remote control! It won't work to hide the batteries any more!

Watch out, this chapter can get sparky!

TOP TIP

OPPOSITES ATTRACT...

Everything is made of atoms. These atoms are made of smaller particles called protons, neutrons and electrons. The protons and neutrons are in the center of each atom (in the nucleus) and the electrons whiz around the outside. Protons are positively charged and electrons are negatively charged. When two objects rub against each other, sometimes electrons are rubbed off one object and onto the other. This makes one object have more electrons and therefore be more negatively charged. The other object has fewer electrons and therefore is more positively charged. Oppositely charged objects will attract each other.

BRIGHT SPARK...

Sometimes when the build up of electrons is great enough, they can jump from one object to another and we see this as a spark, like lightning! You may have felt this when taking off a woolly sweater or after sliding off a car seat and touching the car door.

MAGNETIC FUN

Discover how a magnet works and use it to prove that your breakfast cereal is full of iron! Then get stuck into some magnetic, moving slime.

FRUITY BATTERY!

It's easy to plug in a lamp and send electricity to light it up, or pop a battery into a flashlight to make it shine. But did you know that you can make a light glow by using some fruit, coins, and nails? Get ready for a bright and juicy experiment!

Mix up the lemons with

WHAT YOU NEED

30 minutes

- ☐ 1 each: lemon, lime, and orange
- ☐ 3 copper coins
- ☐ 3 galvanized nails
- ☐ 4 double-ended alligator clip sets
- ☐ small LED light

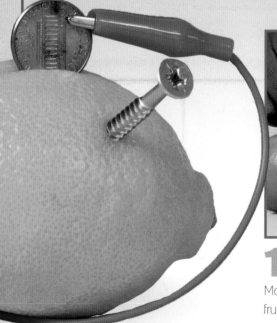

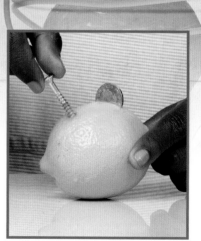

1 Polish the copper coins so they shine (see page 30). Make a small slit in each piece of fruit and push the coin about half way in.

2 Push a galvanized nail about halfway into each piece of fruit. Make sure the coin and the nail do not touch.

3 Take an alligator clip and attach one clip to one nail. Attach the other end to a penny on another piece of fruit.

limes and oranges ... what happens?

If it doesn't work initially, you may need to use more fruit!

TOP TIP

THE SCIENCE STUFF

BRIGHT SPARKS...

A regular battery is made up of two metals, zinc and copper, and an acidic solution. The fruit battery works because its components contain the same materials as a regular battery: the copper coins, the zinc nails, and the citric acid in the fruit. The fruit battery makes an electrical current flow around a circuit with enough energy to light up a small LED light!

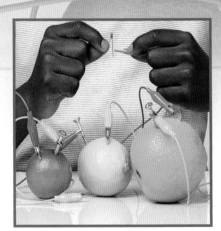

NOW HACK IT!!

⭐ TRY IT!

What happens if you attach the shorter leg of the LED to the coin? Try the same experiment using potatoes. Is the light brighter or dimmer than using the lemons?

4 Connect the other three alligator clips and you will be left with one clip attached to a penny with the other end loose, and one clip attached to a nail with the other end loose.

5 Attach the long leg of the LED to the clip attached to the coin, and the short one to the clip attached to the nail. What happens?

99

GO BANANAS!

The previous activity showed you the power of lemons, limes, and oranges. Let's take the fruity battery experiment to another level. Time to go bananas! Each banana, coin, and screw is one cell. One cell produces a small amount of electricity. Electricity is measured in units of power called "watts." The more "watts," the more power the electricity has and the brighter the light. How many bananas, coins, nails, and clips do you have to use to create a battery that lights up the LED?

Remember to press the buttons on the cover to make an electric circuit and hear sounds!

TOP TIP

30 minutes

WHAT YOU NEED

- ☐ bananas
- ☐ copper coins
- ☐ galvanized nails
- ☐ alligator clip sets
- ☐ small LED light

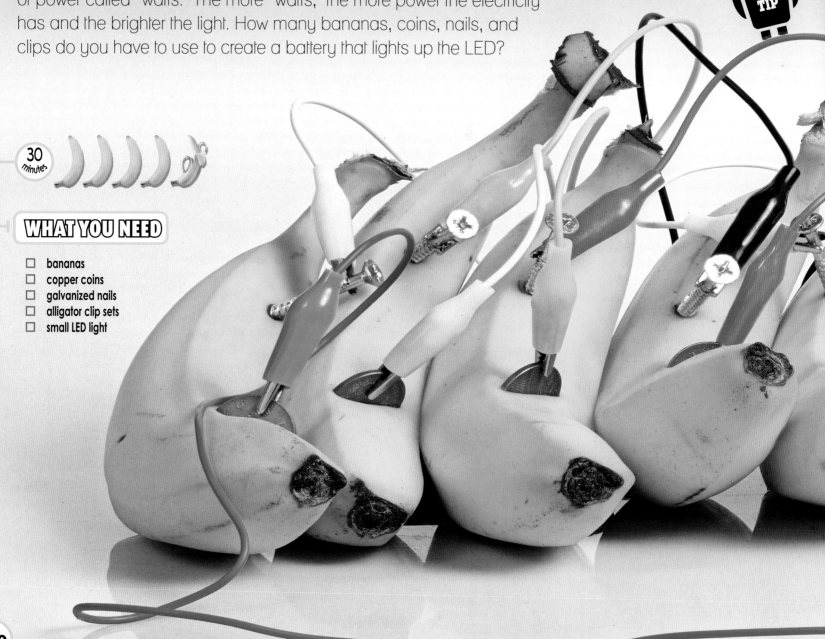

SHORT (OR LONG) CIRCUIT...

A battery has two ends—a positive terminal (the copper coin) and a negative terminal (the zinc nail). If you connect the two terminals with wire, a circuit is formed. Electrons (tiny particles that whiz around atoms) will flow through the wire and a current of electricity is produced.

NOW HACK IT!!

★ TRY THIS!

Can you make the light brighter by adding more bananas? What happens if you use bananas and lemons in the same battery?

101

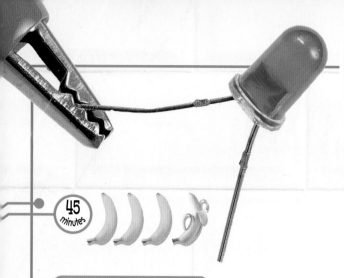

COIN BATTERY

Did you know that you can make a battery with coins? This coin battery will produce a voltage similar to a small regular battery. Try it out. You may have to experiment with how many coins it takes to light up the LED.

45 minutes

Shine the copper coins. See page 30.

WHAT YOU NEED

- 8 copper coins
- cardboard
- pen
- scissors
- aluminum foil
- bowl
- white vinegar

- 1 tsp salt
- tape
- 2 alligator clips, each with a stripped end
- small LED light

TOP TIP

1 Draw around a coin to make eight circles in the cardboard. Cut out the circles. Repeat this on the piece of foil. You should have eight cardboard circles and eight foil ones.

2 Drop the cardboard disks into a bowl. Cover them with vinegar and the salt. Soak the disks so they absorb as much liquid as possible.

3 Lay a coin on the table. Add a soaked cardboard disk and a foil disk on top of the coin. Keep going in that order: coin, cardboard, foil, until you have used them all up.

4 Now make the battery. Lay a length of tape on the table. Attach the stripped end from one alligator clip to the sticky tape. Make sure the naked wire is on the tape.

NOW HACK IT!!

⭐ TRY IT!

Make an even taller battery. Does the light shine brighter as the stack gets higher?

⭐ NOW TRY THIS!

Ask an adult to help you to attach the clips to your remote control. One clip should attach to the positive terminal and one to the negative terminal. Can you control the TV? !!!

THE SCIENCE STUFF

LET IT FLOW...

The vinegar and salt mixture is a liquid that contains electrically charged ions. When the foil and copper coins come into contact with the liquid a reaction takes place that releases electrons. These electrons then flow through the wires connected to the battery and light up the LED.

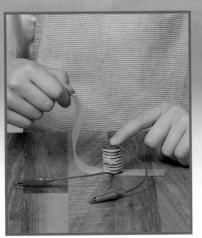

5 Carefully lay your stacked battery on top of the wire. Now lay the loose end of the other wire on top of the stack. Wrap the tape around to hold them in place.

6 Fix the alligator clips to the two arms of the LED light. What happens?

MAKE A PENCIL CIRCUIT

Who would have thought that a simple pencil could make an LED light up? Believe it or not, the graphite in pencils can conduct electricity. In fact, graphite is the only nonmetal that can do this. All you need is a battery, some alligator clips, an LED light, and a penciled line to complete the circuit. Draw your own!

Remember, it's important to spot which is the long leg and short leg of the LED!

TOP TIP

WHAT YOU NEED

45 minutes

- ☐ graphite pencil (e.g. 2B)
- ☐ thick drawing paper
- ☐ alligator clip set (2 leads)
- ☐ 9V battery
- ☐ LED light

1 Use the pencil to draw a rectangle on the paper. Fill in the rectangle heavily. Make sure there are no empty spots.

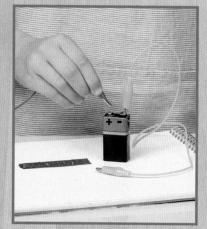

2 Attach two alligator clips to the battery, one on the positive terminal and one on the negative terminal.

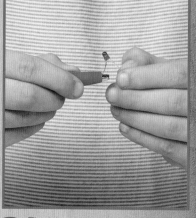

3 Find the alligator clip that is attached to the positive terminal. Take the clip on its other end and attach it to the long leg of the LED light.

4 Hold the negative alligator clip on one end of the graphite rectangle and hold the short end of the LED at the other. What happens?

NOW HACK IT!!

⭐ TRY IT!

Repeat this activity. Except in step 1, fill in the box lightly. Compare the results from the two different rectangles. How are they different? Want to know why? Read about it on page 107.

⭐ NOW TRY THIS!

Draw a really long line. How far apart can you stretch the distance between the clip from the negative terminal and the LED?

THE SCIENCE STUFF

PENCIL ELECTRICITY...

A conductor is a material that allows electricity or heat to flow through it easily. Metals are particularly good conductors, which is why wires are made of metal. Because graphite can carry electrons through it, it is also a very good conductor of electricity. So the graphite completes the electric circuit between the battery and the LED.

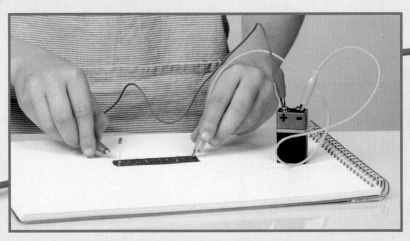

5 Now slide the alligator wire toward the LED light. Does the light get brighter or dimmer?

ROBOT LIGHT!

In the previous activity, you learned how graphite can conduct electricity. Get ready to draw more circuits! Take your graphite pencil and draw a picture to create a circuit! Draw a simple robot picture, making sure you leave a ½ in (1 cm) gap between the finishing points at either end. Go over your lines a few times. Mark one line with a positive (+) and one line with a negative (-) sign at either end. Attach two alligator clips to the battery. Match the wires to the positive and negative symbols on the drawing. Take the LED and bend the legs so it stands up. Place the long leg on the positive line and the short leg on the negative line. Does it light up?

WHAT YOU NEED

45 minutes

- ☐ graphite pencil (eg. 2B)
- ☐ thick drawing paper
- ☐ LED light
- ☐ alligator clip set (2 leads)
- ☐ 9V battery

+ -

Add extra decorations that are not part of the circuit.

There must be no gaps in the lines at all.

Make sure you color in the lines hard.

+ -

Trace or copy this **robot** if that...

...makes things **easier!**

You can buy a selection of different colored LED lights.

NOW HACK IT!!

⭐ TRY IT!

Make your own flashlight by drawing two graphite lines across a piece of card reaching either side. Roll the card into a cone shape. Tape the LED to the wide end making sure one leg is touching each graphite line. Attach two alligator clips to a battery. Attach the other ends to the ends of the graphite lines. Turn the lights off!

THE SCIENCE STUFF

ROBOT FLOW...

The insides of pencils are made largely of clay and graphite. Some pencils have more graphite than others. The higher B number a pencil has, the more graphite it will contain. The graphite carries the electrons through your drawing, whatever shape it is! But the line has to be drawn heavily and can't be too long.

Don't forget to match the clips to the positive and negative terminals

TOP TIP

SUPER CIRCUITS

Computers contain tiny circuit boards that have incredibly complicated electrical or data circuits, which fit on a horizontal layer of cardboard.

STATIC ELECTRICITY

IT'S ZAPTASTIC!

Static electricity happens when an electrical charge builds up on the surface of an object. It's "static" because the charges stay in one area, rather than moving around. Let's make some static electricity!

1 IN A SPIN

Stick a toothpick to a table with some sticky tack. Balance a piece of folded aluminum foil on top. Rub an inflated balloon against your hair so it becomes statically charged. Bring it toward one end of the foil. What does the foil do?

WHO KNEW?

The foil should spin! Rubbing the balloon on your head attracts electrons from your hair. It creates a negative charge. The negatively charged balloon then attracts the positively charged foil, causing it to move.

2 SALT AND PEPPER

Sprinkle some small mounds of salt and pepper onto a plate and mix them up. Rub a balloon onto your hair then hold it over the plate. What happens to the salt and pepper?

WHO KNEW?

Rubbing the balloon on your hair statically charges it. When the balloon gets close to the salt and pepper, you should see (and hear) them move up toward it.

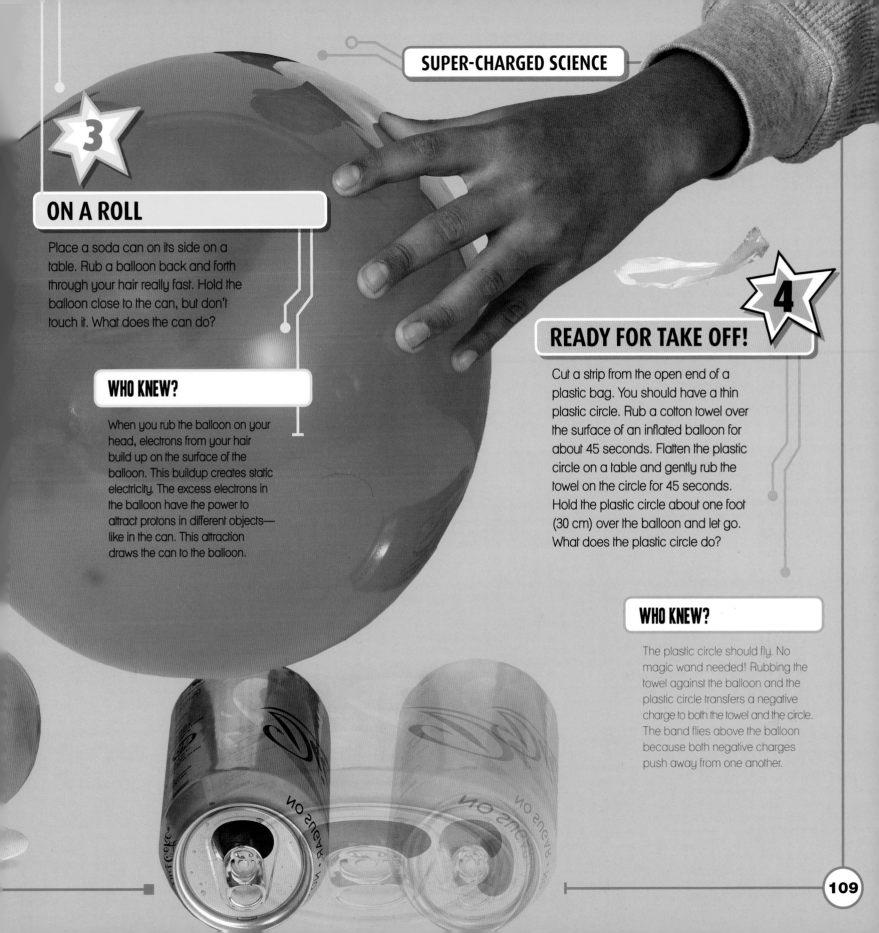

3

ON A ROLL

Place a soda can on its side on a table. Rub a balloon back and forth through your hair really fast. Hold the balloon close to the can, but don't touch it. What does the can do?

WHO KNEW?

When you rub the balloon on your head, electrons from your hair build up on the surface of the balloon. This buildup creates static electricity. The excess electrons in the balloon have the power to attract protons in different objects—like in the can. This attraction draws the can to the balloon.

4

READY FOR TAKE OFF!

Cut a strip from the open end of a plastic bag. You should have a thin plastic circle. Rub a cotton towel over the surface of an inflated balloon for about 45 seconds. Flatten the plastic circle on a table and gently rub the towel on the circle for 45 seconds. Hold the plastic circle about one foot (30 cm) over the balloon and let go. What does the plastic circle do?

WHO KNEW?

The plastic circle should fly. No magic wand needed! Rubbing the towel against the balloon and the plastic circle transfers a negative charge to both the towel and the circle. The band flies above the balloon because both negative charges push away from one another.

STATIC BUTTERFLIES!

Who knew electricity could make butterflies dance? It all has to do with static electricity. This time, all you need is a balloon, a wool sweater, and some tissue paper. Cut some shapes, such as butterflies, out of tissue paper. Natural fibers generate static electricity more easily than human-made fibers, so make sure your sweater is made of pure wool. Rub the balloon up and down the sweater for a few minutes. Now hold the balloon just above the tissue paper and see butterflies fly!

WHAT YOU NEED

10 minutes

- ☐ tissue paper
- ☐ scissors
- ☐ balloon
- ☐ wool sweater

Watch the butterflies fly up and down and up again!

Gently lower the balloon toward the table.

TOP TIP

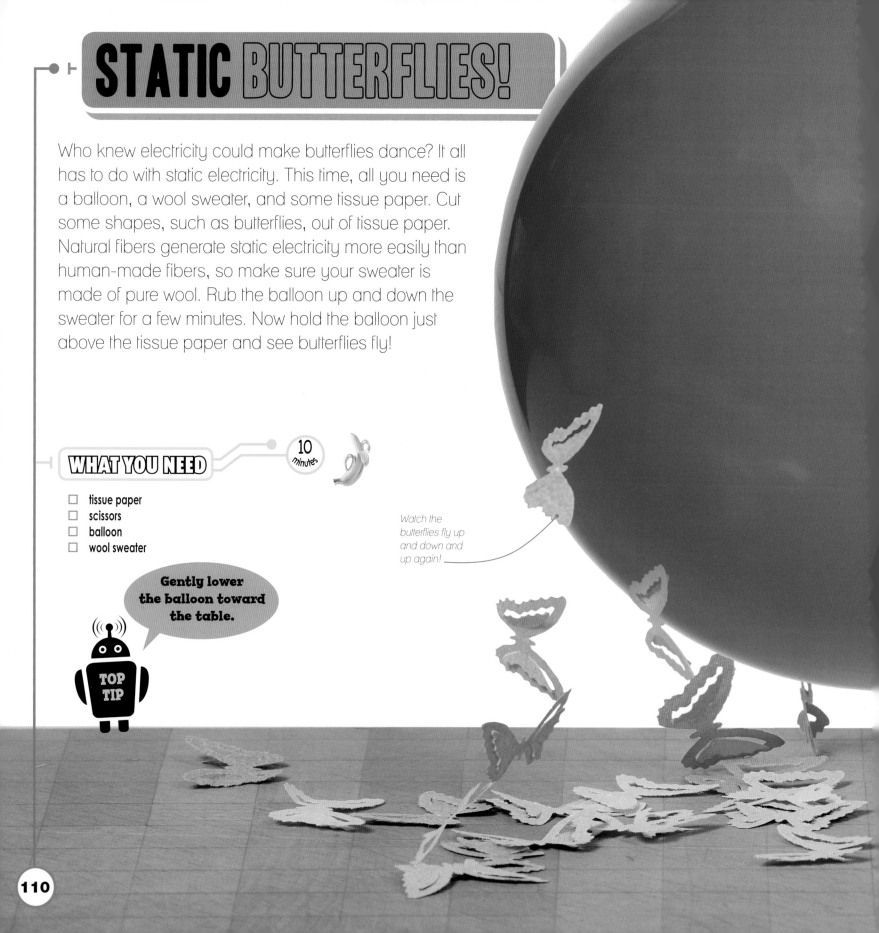

See how many **butterflies** you can **get to fly!**

THE SCIENCE STUFF

SUPER CHARGED BUTTERFLIES...

The rubbing of the balloon against the wool creates an electric charge. The tissue paper is attracted to the charge, and because the tissue paper is so light the charge is enough to lift the butterflies off the table.

MAGNIFICENT MAGNETS

- ☐ neodymium magnets
- ☐ small metal objects such as paperclips, safety pins, and paper fasteners

Have you ever wanted a superpower? Imagine holding up your hand and magically picking up metal objects without handling them? It's all down to magnetism. Not yours of course! Put one superstrong neodymium magnet on top of your hand and find out what materials in your home are attracted to magnets. Create a big pile and see your superpower at work!

Hold your hand steady or the objects will creep around to snap against the magnet!

TOP TIP

THE SCIENCE STUFF

MAGNETIC ATTRACTION...

Magnets have two ends, the north pole and the south pole. Put two magnets together and if the north and south poles are against each other they attract, but if the same poles are together, they repel each other, or push each other away. All materials have some magnetic force, but there are three naturally-occurring ferromagnetic substances that are so strong that you can actually see them working. They are iron, cobalt, and nickel.

The more magnets you use, the stronger the magnetic force will be!

NOW HACK IT!!

★ TRY THIS!

Lay a piece of paper at the bottom of a shoebox. Put a few drops of paint onto the paper. Drop a paper clip inside the box, then hold a magnet underneath the box. Move the magnet around and watch the paperclip paint!

MAKE AN ELECTROMAGNET

Magnets that you stick on the fridge can use their magnetic force without any outside help; they always stick. These are called permanent magnets. Electromagnets, however, only work when electricity is flowing through them. Make your own electromagnet, and see what you can pick up!

WHAT YOU NEED

45 minutes

- ☐ large iron nail, about 3 in (7.5 cm) long
- ☐ 3 ft (90 cm) of thin, coated copper wire
- ☐ small scissors
- ☐ new battery (D size or 9V)
- ☐ tape
- ☐ small magnetic objects such as paperclips

Make sure you cover all of the exposed wire with tape.

TOP TIP

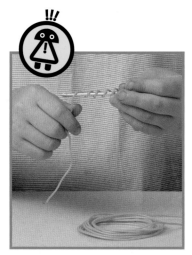

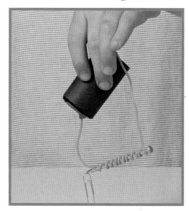

1 Wrap the wire around the nail. Ask an adult to help you snip the coating over the wire with scissors and pull it off, so that about 4 in (10 cm) of wire is exposed at each end.

2 Place one end of the wire onto one end of the battery. Secure into place with the tape. Tape the other end of the wire to the opposite end of the battery.

3 Now you have your electromagnet! Hold the end of the nail to a paperclip. Does it pick it up?

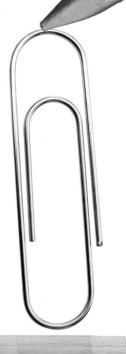

Try picking
up heavier objects.
Does it work?

MAGNETIC POWER

Very large and powerful electromagnets are used as lifting magnets in scrap yards. These electromagnets sort out and pick up iron and steel. When the metals need to be dropped, the magnet can be turned off!

THE SCIENCE STUFF

MAGNETIC PULL...

Metals are made up of lots and lots of tiny little parts called domains. Each of these domains acts like a tiny magnet. All of these domains are jumbled up and point in different directions. However, when they are all lined up and point the same way, they turn the metal magnetic. When the electric current flows through the wire it makes all the domains in the nail line up. Result: magnetic nail!

NOW HACK IT!!

TRY THIS!

Double the number of times you wrap the wire around the nail. Does it make your electromagnet stronger?

NOW TRY THIS!

Try picking up other metals with your electromagnet. Which metals do you think are the most magnetic?

IRON FOR BREAKFAST

Have you ever eaten iron for breakfast? The chances are you probably have! But not nails—cornflakes! Some cornflakes contain iron. Prove this by using a magnet. Pour yourself a bowl and search for the iron!

30 minutes

WHAT YOU NEED

- ☐ bowl of cornflakes (check the ingredients on the box to make sure the cornflakes contain iron)
- ☐ sealable plastic bag
- ☐ pitcher or measuring cup
- ☐ warm water
- ☐ strong magnet

1 Pour the cornflakes into the bag. Use your hands to gently crush the cornflakes. Then use a pitcher or measuring cup to help you fill the bag about 3/4 full with water.

THE SCIENCE STUFF

IRON MAN...

Iron is magnetic. Crushing the cereal and suspending it in water separates the iron from the cereal so that it will attract to the magnet. Cereal often has tiny amounts of iron in it to keep us healthy. Our body needs iron to live. In fact, your body has enough iron in it to make quite a long nail! Most of our iron is in our blood and it helps us to carry oxygen around our body.

NOW HACK IT!!

⭐ TRY THIS!

Try crushing the cornflakes on a plate without adding any water. Hold a strong magnet, wrapped in kitchen plastic wrap, toward the cornflakes. Do any of the flakes rise up toward the magnet?

⭐ NOW TRY THIS!

Check out some other cereals. Can you extract more iron from another type?

> Once the magnet is on the bag, don't move the magnet or the iron pieces will fall away.

TOP TIP

2 Seal the bag shut. Then shake it for about one minute. What's inside the bag should turn into a mushy, cornflake soup!

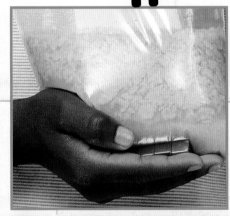

3 With one hand, hold the magnet to the bottom of the bag. Use your other hand to hold the top of the bag. With your hands firmly in place, move the bag in a circular motion for about 30 seconds.

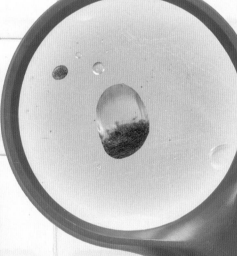

4 Carefully flip the bag upside down. (Do NOT let go of the magnet!) The soupy cornflakes should now be at the bottom. Now look under the magnet. Do you see black specks? That's the iron!

MAGNETIC SLIME

Remember all the slime you made back on page 44? Well now it's time to make some extreme slime! This one can dance! Amaze your friends by making a slime that simply looks like it has glitter in it, but magically moves all by itself! Watch your slime stretch, wiggle, and twist!

The stronger the magnet, the better the stretch. Try a neodymium magnet.

TOP TIP

1 Make up a batch of slime from page 44.

2 Pour the iron filings into your bowl of slime. Stir them in well. Pour the slime out onto a flat surface.

3 Make your slime move! Put the magnet close to the slime and then move the magnet around.

WHAT YOU NEED

30 minutes

- ☐ slime from page 44
- ☐ 1 tbsp iron filings
- ☐ spoon or stirrer
- ☐ strong magnet

THE SCIENCE STUFF

MAGNETIC FIGHT...

The slime polymer molecules are held by cohesion—that's the force that holds molecules of the same type together. The slime holds onto the iron filings because of adhesion. This is a force that holds molecules of a different type together. The magnet is attracted to the iron filings and tries to pull them out, but adhesion and cohesion keep the iron filings in the slime. That fight creates the stretching and dancing!

NOW HACK IT!!

 TRY THIS!

First of all, hold the magnet close without touching the slime. It's quite tricky! Watch the slime stretch toward it. What happens if you drop the magnet into the slime?

NOW TRY THIS!

Try putting other magnetic materials into the slime rather than the iron filings. Does it work if you put paperclips into it?

GLOSSARY

Here's a list of the all the science-y words you will find in this book, along with an explanation of what they mean.

ACIDS
A sour, and sometimes destructive, chemical substance that appears in many household products like foods, cleaning products, and batteries, as well as in the human body. It has a low pH level unlike its chemical opposite, bases.

ADHESION
An intermolecular force that makes molecules cling to the solid surface of a substance. It is the reason why water spreads upward on a piece of paper when it gets wet.

AIR RESISTANCE
A frictional force that moves against a falling object to slow it down. It is the force that slows the descent of skydivers when their parachute opens.

ATOMS
The smallest unit of all matter that makes up everything. They contain three smaller particles; protons (which are positively charged), neutrons (which have no charge), and electrons (which are negatively charged).

BASES
A family of chemicals that are sometimes destructive, which appear in many household cleaning products, foods, and batteries. They have a pH greater than 7 and feel soapy to the touch.

CAPILLARY ACTION
The upward movement of liquids through small holes. The action occurs through the combined forces of adhesion, cohesion, and surface tension.

CARBON DIOXIDE
A colorless, odorless gas, which is produced by burning fossil fuels as well as in respiration by animals and plants. Importantly, plants use this gas to make glucose in the process of photosynthesis.

CELLS
The building block of all living things. A group of similar cells is called a tissue and a group of tissues make an organ. Some life forms, like bacteria, are made of just a single cell. Humans, however, contain about 37.2 trillion cells!

CHEMICAL REACTION
The process of rearranging atoms in one or more substances (reactants) to form something different (products), for example when iron rusts or wood burns.

CHLOROPHYLL
A green pigment found in the chloroplasts of plant cells (and also some photosynthetic bacteria). Chlorophyll absorbs sunlight, which provides the energy for the process of photosynthesis. This process uses carbon dioxide and water to make oxygen and glucose.

CIRCUIT
The path that electric current flows through. The charge flows from the positive side of a cell or battery to the negative side of a cell or battery.

COHESION
An intermolecular force that causes alike molecules to cling to each other. It is the reason why water molecules cling together to form dew drops.

COMPOUND
A substance made from two or more elements chemically bonded together. Examples include water and salt.

CONDUCTION
The transfer of heat or electricity from one area to another.

DENSITY
A measure of how close the particles are together in a substance. It is found by dividing the mass of an object by its volume.

DISPLACEMENT
The physical process of water being pushed out of the way by an object when it is immersed in water. The volume of water that is pushed out of the way is equal to the volume of the object in the water.

DISSOLVE
When a solid or a gas is incorporated into a liquid to form a solution.

ECOSYSTEM
The living organisms and non-living aspects of a certain area. For example a forest ecosystem includes all the plants, bacteria, fungi, and animals as well as non-living features, such as the type of soil, rocks, and temperature of the area.

ELECTRIC CURRENT
The flow of electrical charge from the positive side of a cell/battery to the negative side of a cell/battery. When current flows through a bulb it lights up.

ELECTRICITY
The flow of charged particles, such as electrons or ions.

ELECTROMAGNET
A magnet that can be switched on and off. It is made of a core (usually soft iron) with wire coiled around it. When electricity flows through the wire, the core becomes magnetized.

ELECTRONS
A fundamental particle that is part of an atom. Electrons are negatively charged and are involved in chemical bonding.

ELEMENTS
A substance made of only one type of atom.

ENZYME
A chemical made by a living organism that speeds up the rate of reactions taking place in and around cells. For example, digestive enzymes break down big, insoluble molecules such as starch, into smaller soluble molecules, such as glucose, which can be absorbed.

EVAPORATION
The gradual process of turning a liquid into a gas, just like a puddle of water evaporates and turns into water vapor on a warm, sunny day.

EXPERIMENT
A test to understand or discover a scientific idea. It usually includes a question, hypothesis, and conclusion.

FORCE
A push or a pull that will cause an object to change speed, direction, or change shape. A force can be caused when two objects touch each other or without touching (like gravity or magnetism).

FREEZING POINT
The temperature at which a liquid turns into a solid, like when water turns into ice. Different liquids freeze at different temperatures.

GAS
A state of matter (like liquid or solid), where the particles are very fast moving and spread far apart. A gas will fill the space of the container it is placed in, like helium filling a balloon.

GEODE
Plain rocks with crystals inside them. Usually found in deserts and volcanic areas, these rocks are made over the course of thousands of years when dissolved minerals trapped in rocks crystallize over time as the water escapes.

GERMINATE
One of the first steps in the life cycle of a plant, it is the process in which a seed begins to sprout and grow.

GLUCOSE
A type of sugar that is used by living organisms for the process of respiration. Respiration uses glucose to release energy that is used for other reactions in living organisms. Humans get glucose from the food we eat. The glucose is absorbed from the intestine into the blood and then transported to all our cells.

GRAVITY
A force of attraction that affects all objects by pulling them together. The force pulls harder on heavier objects, but less on objects that are far from each other. This is the reason why humans stay on the ground while on Earth.

INDICATOR
A substance that changes color depending on the pH of the solution it is in.

INSOLUBLE
The property of something that will not dissolve in a solvent.

ION
A charged particle. A bit like an atom or a molecule that has lost one or more electrons to become positively charged, or has gained one or more electrons to become negatively charged.

LIQUID

A state of matter (like solid and gas) where the particles are arranged randomly. The particles move and flow together to fill the bottom of the container they are placed in.

MAGNETIC POLE

The parts of the magnet with the strongest pull. All magnets have a north pole and a south pole. Opposite poles attract and like poles repel.

MASS

The measurement of the amount of matter that an object holds calculated based on its density and volume. It never changes despite the forces that may be applied to it.

MELTING POINT

The temperature at which a solid turns into a liquid. The melting point of pure ice is 0°C. Different solids melt at different temperatures.

MEMBRANE

A thin layer around the edge of an object. All living cells are surrounded by a membrane. Eggs also have a membrane under the shell and around the egg white.

MICROBES/MICROORGANISM

Living organisms that are too small to see with the naked eye. Microbes include bacteria and some types of fungi. Some microbes can cause disease, but other microbes, such as yeast, are very useful for us.

MOLECULE

Two or more atoms bonded together. Some molecules contain only two atoms, like oxygen (O_2). DNA, on the other hand, contains roughly 2 billion atoms!

NEUTRAL

A substance that is neither acidic nor basic, such as water. At room temperature these substances have a pH of 7.

NON-NEWTONIAN FLUID

Fluids that change properties based on the amount of stress applied to them, like dough or quicksand. A fluid whose properties aren't like other fluids.

ORGANISM

An individual life form such as a particular type of plant, animal, bacteria, or fungus.

OSMOSIS

The movement of water molecules through a semipermeable membrane (from a more concentrated solution to a less concentrated solution). Plants often absorb water from the soil by osmosis.

OXIDATION

A reaction that occurs when oxygen is added to something to form a new compound. One example of this is when iron reacts with oxygen in the air to form rust.

OXYGEN

A colorless, tasteless, and odorless gas that is found in the Earth's atmosphere and crust. It is the third most abundant element in the universe.

PARTICLE

The smallest piece of matter possible that makes up all of the things in the universe. Individual bits of these substances cannot be seen by the human eye.

PHOTOSYNTHESIS

A process that occurs in plants (and some bacteria). It uses the energy from light, carbon dioxide from the air, and water to make glucose and oxygen. The glucose is used to make all the molecules needed to live and grow.

POLYMER

A large molecule made by joining lots of small molecules, called monomers, together. These exist naturally in things like proteins and silk. Human-made polymers are also made, such as polyester and plastics.

POROUS

A solid containing small holes that could let gases and liquids in or out.

POWER

A measure of the amount of energy transferred in a given amount of time. The standard unit of power is the Watt.

PRESSURE

A measured amount of exertion that causes different reactions depending on the amount of force and the overall surface area it's applied to.

RESPIRATION
Respiration is a chemical reaction that happens in all living cells to release energy. This energy is used to power most other processes necessary for living and growing.

SOLID
A state of matter (like liquid and gas). In a solid, all the particles are regularly arranged and very close together. The particles vibrate about fixed points. A solid cannot change its shape unless a force is applied to it.

SOLUBLE
The property of something that will dissolve in a given solvent.

SOLUTION
A mixture that is formed when a solute dissolves in a solvent. Salt water is an example of a solution. The solute, salt, has dissolved in the solvent, water.

STALACTITE
Mineral formations that "grow" down from the ceiling of caves. The formations are created by water containing minerals dripping from the ceiling and as the water evaporates, it leaves the minerals behind.

STATIC ELECTRICITY
The build-up of charge on an object, either by adding electrons to it, or removing electrons from it. This only happens when there is nowhere for the electrons to flow (like on an insulator). It can be used to explain why a balloon will attract your hair once you have rubbed the balloon on it.

SURFACE AREA
The amount of space on the outside of an object.

SURFACE TENSION
The attractive force at the surface of a liquid that minimises the surface area and creates a tight layer of particles. It's this force that allows very small objects, like insects or a paperclip, to float on the top of the water.

TRANSPIRATION
The loss of water from leaves by evaporation. This causes more water to be drawn up through the roots, to replace the water that has been lost.

VOLTAGE
More correctly known as *potential difference*. This is the amount of force that pushes electrons around an electrical circuit. The greater the voltage, the more force behind the electrons. The unit of voltage is the Volt.

VOLUME
The amount of three-dimensional space a solid, liquid, or gas occupies.

WATT
The unit of electrical power. One Watt is one Joule of energy transferred in one second.

INDEX

CREDITS

PICTURE CREDITS

Photos ©: Alamy Images: 27 bl (David Dugle), 26-27 r (Martin Shields); iStockphoto: 86 r (101cats), 59 br (AlasdairJames), 30 tl (almagami), 70-71 bg (Andreealonascu), 9 cl (ANGHI), 9 cr (Aslan Alphan), 115 tr (BanksPhotos), 104 tl (boschettophotography), 10 bl and throughout (bubaone), 46 b spread (BWFolsom), 88 cr (camacho9999), 38 tr (Cipariss), 76 cl (ConstantinosZ), 59 c (danako), 26-27 t spread (dkidpix), 59 bc (domnicky), 90 t spread (draganab), 71 cl and br (duckycards), 88 c and throughout (duckycards), 99 br (duckycards), 108 cr (Elenathewise), 88 cl (fabiofoto), 70 b spread (fcafotodigital), 39 tl (Floortje), 81 br (FreedomMaster), 38 tc (GeoffBlack), 10 l, c and throughout (harmpeti), 89 cr (hayatikayhan), 88 tr (jakrin1976), 18-19 spread (joel-t), 28 tl and throughout (keport), 87 br (KjellBrynildsen), 89 br (Lemon_tm), 11 tr and throughout (LysenkoAlexander), 36 c (MarkGillow), 107 cb (mattjeacock), 90 spread b (MichaelJay), 43 r (mijastrzebski), 65 cr (mingman), 42 tr (Nastco), 114 br (pixhook), 87 br (ranasu), 83 tl (RuslanDashinsky), 30 cr (rusm), 81 cr (SerrNovik), 38 c (showcake), 87 br (slavadubrovin), 16 b spread and throughout (sommaiphoto), 89 br (srdjan111), 27 c (studiocasper), 76 c (Talaj), 30 cl (TonyBaggett), 10 r and throughout (unalozmen), 86 br (ValentynVolkov), 22 tl (vectorplusb), 14 tl and throughout (Vijay Patel), 64 br (VitaliiPhoto), 21 tl (wabeno), 7 cl (Yun Heng Lin); Shutterstock: 24 tl (simonidadj), 65 l (don padungvichean), 64 cr (Elena Zajchikova), 61 r (IrinaK), 64 bc (Photography by Adri), 106 bl (pticelov), 59 bl (Richard Griffin), 7 cr (Stephane Bidouze), 32 r (WINS86), 86 bl (Zhukov Oleg); 33 t, 52-53 t spread (sky), 125 br (bigmetalfish); all other images by Scholastic Inc.

ACKNOWLEDGEMENTS

Thanks to: Penny Arlon, Tory Gordon-Harris, Julia Sabbagh, John Goldsmid, and Sunita Gahir.

BATTERY INFORMATION

Book Battery Diagram
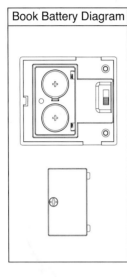

IMPORTANT BATTERY INFORMATION!
KEEP LOOSE BATTERIES AWAY FROM YOUNG CHILDREN! Please retain for future reference.
- Book: Use 2 x LR1130 batteries only. 1.5v.
- Battery installation and removal should be performed by an adult.

To remove or insert batteries, use a screwdriver to loosen the safety screw on the battery compartment door. Screw does not separate from door. Lift and remove door. Take out and safely dispose of old batteries. Follow polarity diagram inside battery compartment to insert two new LR1130 1.5v batteries only. Put battery compartment door back and secure safety screw. Do not use excess force or improper type or size of screwdriver.

- Use only batteries recommended in this instruction manual.
- Only batteries of the same or equivalent types as recommended are to be used.
- Be careful to install batteries with the correct polarity, as indicated.
- Remove exhausted batteries.
- Remove all batteries when replacing.
- Do not mix old and new batteries.
- Do not mix alkaline, standard, rechargeable, or different types of batteries.
- Non-rechargeable batteries are not to be recharged.
- Rechargeable batteries are only to be charged under adult supervision (if removable).
- Rechargeable batteries are to be removed from the toy before being charged.
- The supply terminals are not to be short-circuited.
- CAUTION: Do not dispose of battery in fire. Battery may explode.

RENSEIGNEMENTS IMPORTANTS AU SUJET DES PILES
GARDER LES PILES EN VRAC HORS DE LA PORTÉE DES JEUNES ENFANTS! À garder pour référence ultérieure.
- Livre: Utilisez uniquement 2 piles LR1130. 1,5v.
- L'installation et le retrait de la batterie doivent être effectués par un adulte.

LIVRE: Pour retirer les piles ou en insérer, dévisser la vis de sécurité du compartiment à piles. Soulever le couvercle et le retirer. Veuillez noter que la vis reste sur le couvercle. Enlever les piles usées et les recycler de façon appropriée. Insérer 2 piles LR1130 neuves de 1,5v en respectant la polarité indiquée à l'intérieur du compartiment à piles. Remettre le couvercle et la vis en place. Utiliser un tournevis de la taille et du type requis et ne pas serrer trop fort.

- N'utiliser que les piles recommandées dans ce manuel d'instructions.
- N'utiliser que des piles de types identiques ou équivalents à ceux recommandés.
- S'assurer de bien installer les piles en respectant la polarité indiquée.
- Retirer les piles déchargées.
- Retirer toutes les piles au moment du remplacement.
- Ne pas utiliser des piles neuves et usagées en même temps.
- Ne pas mélanger des piles alcalines, standard, rechargeables ou de types différents.
- Ne pas recharger des piles non rechargeables.
- Un adulte doit être présent lors du chargement de piles rechargeables.
- Retirer les piles rechargeables du jouet avant de les recharger.
- Ne pas court-circuiter les points d'échange.
- ATTENTION: Ne pas jeter les piles au feu. Risque d'explosion.